Landmark Visi

Riga & its beaches

Farrol Kahn

Farrol Kahn is an author and has written several books on aviation medicine. He lives in Oxford where he heads The Aviation Health Institute.

Acknowledgements

The author would like to thank the numerous people and institutions who have made the writing of this book possible.

It began with the Ministry of Culture and the Latvian Tourism Development Agency. Karina Pétersone, Minister of Culture was an enthusiastic supporter of the initiative and in spite of her busy schedule wrote a splendid foreword to the book.

Anda Rezgale and later Aivars Kalnins opened many doors for me and have been most generous with their time and help at the Tourist Office.

I was fortunate in meeting Vaira Vike-Freiberga before her election as President of the Republic of Latvia when she was the Director of the Latvian Institute and assisted me with the national cultural treasure of Dainas of which she is the world authority. To her I am extremely grateful.

At the London Latvian Embassy I would like to thank H E Normans Penke, Eva Staltmane, Irena Hamilton and Juris Bone.

There are many others to whom I am specially grateful: Knuts Skujenieks, Janis Borgs, Agnes Rudzite, Solveiga Freiberga, Dale Lawrence, Natalya Krasnopeyeve, Inguna Bakuradze, Ineta Petersone, Vita Jermolovica, Ilze Martinsone, Ieva Lesinska, Anda Vilka, Leva Iltnere, Inta Ruka, Anita Zabilevska, Gatins Kokins, Juris Kapralis, Irena Bakule, Vilnis Smits, Mairita Brice, Liga Libarte, Sarah Bruce Jones, Lilita Laine, Raimonds Auskaps, Neil Taylor, Arija Vanaga, Julia and Maud Rosenthal.

Published by

Landmark Publishing
Ashbourne Hall, Cokayne Ave, Ashbourne,
Derbyshire DE6 1EJ England

Foreword

By Helena Demakova, Latvian Minister of Culture

Proposed Latvian National Library

She is a graduate of the University of Latvia and a talented linguist who speaks Latvian, Russian, English and German perfectly and French adequately. She has had extensive experience in cultural issues and has acted as an advisor to both the minstry of Culture and to the Prime Minister. Her political activities have also been considerable and she is a founding member of the Peoples' Party and was first elected to the Latvian parliament in 1998.

Projects of the 21st Century.

Exciting cultural projects which are planned for the 21st century include a National Library, a Museum of Contemporary Art and a Concert Hall and involve top international architects such as Gunnars Birkets and Rem Koolhaas.

The Latvian National Library will be a multi-functional cultural and educational centre and a depository of knowledge with access to the state of art services. The building which is designed by Birkerts is sited on the left bank of the Daugava opposite the Old Town. The completion date is expected to be in autumn 2008 and the costs will be around 90 million latts.

The Museum of Contemporary Art with an exhibition space of 4,000 square metres will be part of a development that consists of a conference hall, a cinema, a computerised information centre, a library and archives. Space will also be allocated for art education and workshops. The centrepiece of the project is the former power station, located in the Riga port area, which will be integrated by Koolhaas in the new structure. Conservation of the old building and the industrial and historical heritage will be taken into consideration. The development which is estimated to cost 19 million latts and is expected to be completed at the end of 2009, brings to mind Herzog & De Meuron's concept for the Tate Modern.

The Concert Hall which will comprise of two auditoria, a large hall with 1,500 seats and another with 400 seats is to be sited on the Duagava River dam opposite the Old Town. The architects are SZK, a local firm, which has conceived that the building will consist of 12 dark and clustered rectangle and cubic buildings. It will be the new home of the Latvian National Symphony orchestra, the State Academic Choir 'Latvija' and a chamber orchestra. The estimated construction costs are 22 million latts and the date of completion is undecided.

The State Cultural Capital Foundation (CCF) was established in 1998 to provide financial support and promote creative work. To promote its work, there are four competitions a year in 8 fields including cultural heritage and interdisciplinary projects. It has a budget of about 5 million latts a year.

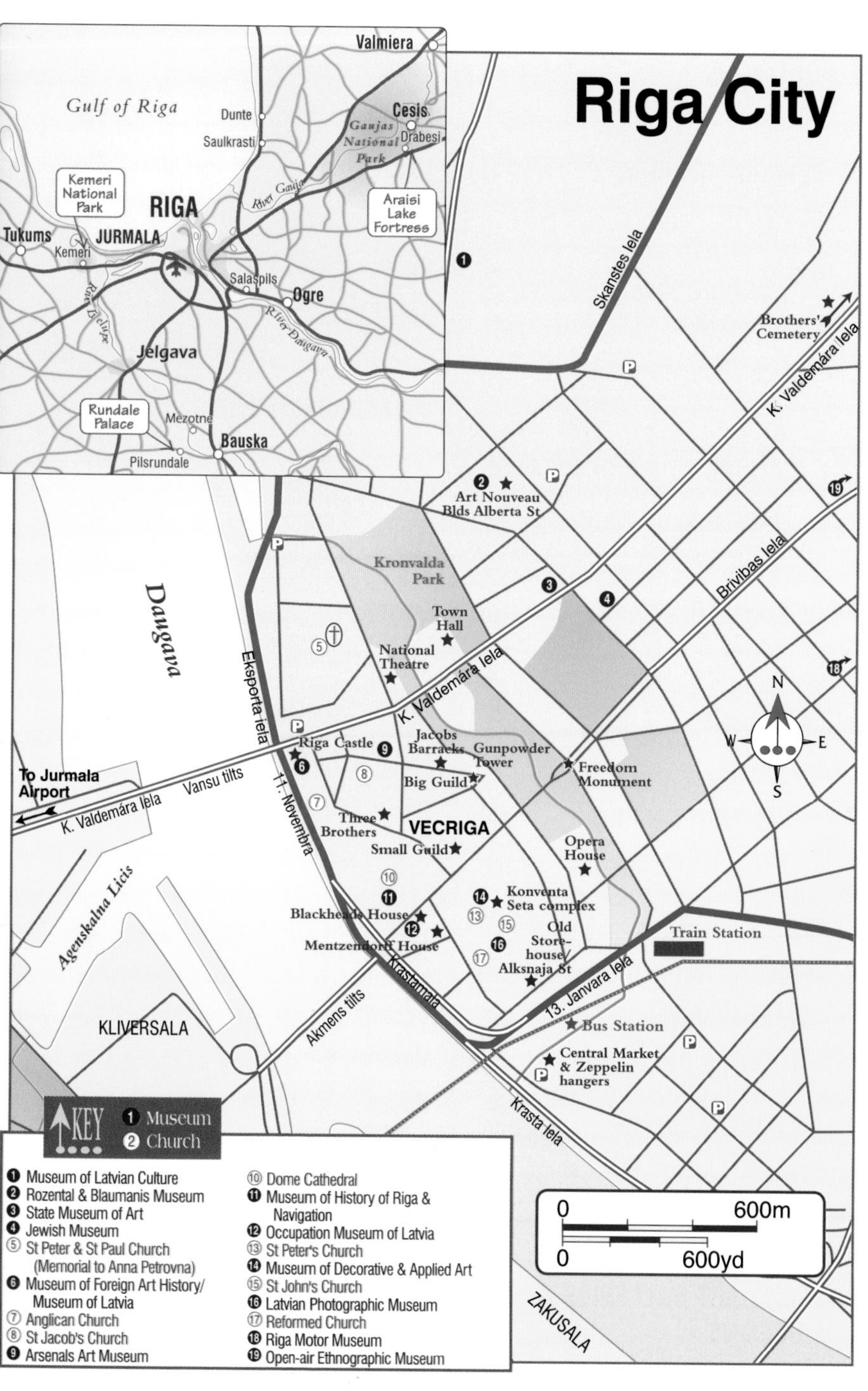
Riga City
Gulf of Riga
Valmiera
Dunte
Saulkrasti
Cesis
Gaujas National Park
Drabesi
River Gauja
Kemeri National Park
RIGA
Araisi Lake Fortress
Tukums
JURMALA
Kemeri
Salaspils
Ogre
River Lielupe
River Daugava
Jelgava
Rundale Palace
Mezotne
Bauska
Pilsrundale
Skanstes Iela
Brothers' Cemetery
K. Valdemára Iela
Art Nouveau Blds Alberta St
Kronvalda Park
Brivibas Iela
Town Hall
National Theatre
Dangava
Eksporta iela
K. Valdemára Iela
Riga Castle
Jacobs Barracks
Gunpowder Tower
Freedom Monument
To Jurmala Airport
Vansu tilts
K. Valdemára Iela
11. Novembra
Big Guild
Three Brothers
VECRIGA
Small Guild
Opera House
Agenskalna Licis
Konventa Seta complex
Blackheads House
Old Store-house/ Alksnaja St
Mentzendorff House
Train Station
Krastanala
13. Janvara iela
Akmens tilts
Bus Station
KLIVERSALA
Central Market & Zeppelin hangers
Krasta Iela
KEY
1 Museum
2 Church
0 600m
0 600yd
ZAKUSALA
N
W
E
S
1 Museum of Latvian Culture
2 Rozental & Blaumanis Museum
3 State Museum of Art
4 Jewish Museum
5 St Peter & St Paul Church (Memorial to Anna Petrovna)
6 Museum of Foreign Art History/ Museum of Latvia
7 Anglican Church
8 St Jacob's Church
9 Arsenals Art Museum
10 Dome Cathedral
11 Museum of History of Riga & Navigation
12 Occupation Museum of Latvia
13 St Peter's Church
14 Museum of Decorative & Applied Art
15 St John's Church
16 Latvian Photographic Museum
17 Reformed Church
18 Riga Motor Museum
19 Open-air Ethnographic Museum

Contents

Feature Boxes

Welcome to

Riga & its beaches

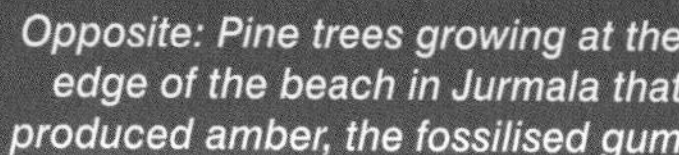

Opposite: Pine trees growing at the edge of the beach in Jurmala that produced amber, the fossilised gum

Riga is a rare discovery in a world that is rapidly running out of new destinations and I certainly did not set out to find such a place, as Robert Byron did in his quest for Oxiana. My father had come from a nearby town, Jelgava (which was then known as Mitau), and I had embarked on a trip to find my roots at the suggestion of a friend.

The city had 'hidden itself', first under the Russian and then under the Soviet sphere of influence, until the last century when Latvia attained Independence for two decades from 1918 to 1940. However, through the secret Molotov-Ribbentrop Pact of August 23rd, 1939, the country was assigned to the Soviet Union and occupied until the early nineties.

Top Tips

1. Old Town(Vevriga)

Located on the eatern side of the Daugava river, it is steeped in history from the German crusader castle to the city's very origins in Konventa Seta where the Grey Sisters, a Franciscan order, had a hospital and Jacob's barracks which was bulit during the Swedish occupation in the 17th century when Riga was the largest city in Sweden.

2. Art Nouveau

One of the secrets of the city are the several hundred buildings in this architectural style which have remained unknown until Latvia regained its independence in 1991.

3.Shopping

Although Riga has a good selection of shops as any other European city including top brand names, some of them are outstanding and unique. There are soaps that smell and look good enough to eat (Stenders);modern linen stylish enough for Giorgio Armani and Calvin Klein to put in their collections (Garage);a paradise for jaded foodies who will find something to titillate their palates in the delicatessen market (Gastronome); and chunky, outre jewelry from top Latvian artists (Putti).

4.Spas

Discover what the Scandinavians and Russians have known for some time, the Spa and health resort of Jurmala. The area which has a separate municipality from Riga has 30 mineral water springs and also special sapropelic mud for slimming treatments. The bonus of a visit is that the facilities are at the seaside where pine forest border on fine sandy beaches.

During the sensitive period of Perestroika, the Prime Minister of the UK, John Major, played a significant role in ensuring that the Baltic States gained independence, according to a former Latvian ambassador to the Soviet Union, Janis Peters.

On a visit to Moscow, John Major committed a breach of Protocol by first inviting the three representatives from Estonia, Latvia and Lithuania to a meeting before seeing President Gorbachov. He sounded them on their views of Independence and when they affirmed their strong interest, he pushed the Soviet Union to acknowledge their constitutional rights. Formal recognition took place on 24th August, 1991. However, for most people in the West, Latvia does not exist or at a guess they would indicate it is part of the Russian republic, which is a great shame and loss to them.

Tacitus was the first to put the country on the map for the Romans when he wrote about the people in his ethnographical work, Germania. He had little to say about these Latvian tribes, who were closer to the Prussians with whom they shared the Indo-European language, but it was startling enough.

The Gulf of Riga he described as a tame, stagnant body of water with a resemblance to parts of the Mediterranean. It marked an important boundary of the earth, because of the phenomenon of the midnight sun which provided a brilliance, that according to him, even dimmed the stars.

He called the people the Aestii, and praised them for their diligence and determination, compared to the indolent Germans who did not cultivate their crops with the same zeal. The Aestii or the Balts were distinguished from other tribes because they were the only people who harvested glaesum or amber from the sea. But as barbarians, they never understood its ornamental worth nor did they enquire about its origins. The Romans had of course, and even burnt the fossil gum to test its properties.

Riga is a place that Pushkin dreamt of visiting as his greatest love, Anna Petrovna Kern, resided there with her husband. It was the period when his infatuation for her turned into a powerful passion and he desperately longed to be with her. But the Tsar, who had exiled him to his estate at Mikhailovskoe, had forbidden travel to the city. Instead, Pushkin cooled his heels and wrote his best love poem, *K.*

In the early 1800s, Riga was on the provincial music circuit in Central Europe and Richard Wagner spent two seminal years in the city. When he left he was determined to stop this itinerant lifestyle, partly caused by fleeing from creditors and had conceived the grandiose idea of Bayreuth, which would be supported by a wealthy patron.

Johann Gottfried von Herder, the German poet and philosopher had a brief sojourn in the city.

In the 1930s it was the place to hang around if you were interested in communists and spies or both, as it was the window to the Soviet Union. George Kennan from the US State Department was here as was the author Graham Greene who was credited with calling it 'Parisian' or 'Paris of the North'. John F Kennedy also turned up as a twenty-two year-old student just before the World War II and there is a plaque on the house he stayed in at 22 Ausekla Street.

From a cultural focal point, Riga has produced leading figures like the film director, Sergei Eisenstein, the philosopher, Isaiah Berlin, the US philanthropist Joseph Hirshhorn and the ballet star, Mikhail Baryshnikov. The city is a cocktail of architectural styles from crusader castles to Renaissance; Gothic cathedrals and Classicism; to the finest examples of Art Nouveau which few Westerners have seen as they have been omitted from reference books.The latter have now been added to Unesco's World Cultural Heritage List.

There always has been a strong British connection since the eighteenth century, mostly through trade. One of the best mayors, George Armistead's forebears came from Yorkshire. More recently the BBC Proms commissioned Peteris Vasks to write a symphony. Football star Marian Pahar was recruited to play for Southampton and top coach Gary Johnson, from Watford, now manages the Latvian National Team.

Hedonists also have a wide choice of activities from beaches to night clubs. The beach coastline, which stretches over 25 miles (40km) and in parts resembles the wild African coast because of the lack of high-rise hotel development, with trees growing near the water-line, has been recommended by no less a figure than the poet, Osip Mandelstam. 'It is famed for its oozy, pure yellow and astonishingly fine sand (even in an hourglass one could hardly find such sand!)' he exclaimed in what could appear to be as inadvertent advertising copy.

While you lie on this 'yellow finely milled canary sand,' no pesky beach salesperson will accost you out of your holiday reverie, and if you walk long enough you will find the only ice-cream cart vendor.There are amazing examples of wooden dachas all over the coast, including the most recent little masterpiece of the top German architect, Meinhard von Gerkan.

Sybarites will find satisfaction at the several spa hotels where they can indulge in mud baths and mineral water massages.The night club scene is as sophisticated as the Parisian Moulin Rouge and caters for all ages, including teeny boppers.An added inducement is that the city is celebrated for the special beauty of its girls who tend to be fashioned like top models, but statuesque and they outnumber the men by two to one.

The food and beer will also excite the palate as there is a latter-day Conran on site and a surprising number of good restaurants. Forget Munich or Prague for the beerfest and come here to try the range of ales in a city where they are so good that you can drink them between courses instead of wine. You can also try Stalin's preferred beer, Rigas Originalais, which incidentally has a very bitter aftertaste.

I never did find traces of our family in Jelgava, because I discovered this Parisian city instead. As a new destination for the twenty-first century, Riga is second to none. It has sea, sun, sand, culture, music, art and is the repository of about three million Dainas or folk songs. And it is cheap. What more can one expect from a capital city.

General

Riga, which is the capital of Latvia, is situated at the south-eastern extremity of the Gulf of Riga in 57°3'N, 24°1'E, with a cosmopolitan population of some 900,000 comprising forty-seven per cent Russians, thirty-eight per cent Latvians, nine per cent Belarussians and Ukranians, and two per cent Poles. The city extends to both banks of the Daugava River, and like Paris there is a right bank where the old town of Vecriga is and a left bank, the Pardaugava, with the tall television tower.

History

Latvia was unknown to Europe until 1158 when Bremen Merchants on a trading mission to Wisby in Gotland Island were shipwrecked on the Gulf of Riga near the mouth of the Daugava River. They formed a settlement on the sandy peninsula between the Daugava and its small tributary the Ridzene from which Riga derives its name. The river was filled in over a century ago although the river bed is still visible.

Riga Central Station

The Middle Ages

In 1201, Bishop Albert who had come to convert the inhabitants to Christi-

Spectaular sunset on one of Riga's many beaches

Jomas street in Majori

anity founded the town and made it the seat of the Bishop of Livonia according to the chro- nicle of Henricus Livonicus. He established a colony with German settlers, established the Dome School in 1211, and founded the Crusader Order of the Brothers of the Sword which joined with the Teutonic Order of Prussia in 1237, known as the Livonian Order.

Riga acquired great privileges and possessions and in 1282 joined the Hanseatic League, adopting the Hamburg code before the end of the thirteenth century. There was constant friction between the archbishops, citizens and knights, which sometimes resulted in pitched battles in which the two former parties united against the third, that generally maintained the upper hand.

As the city grew in prosperity, Guilds were established in 1330 for craftsmen and merchants. In 1522 Riga embraced the tenets of the Reformation and in 1541 joined the League of Schmal-

Sailing on the Lielupe River, Jurmala

Berga Bazars

Berga Bazars which is one of the most interesting shopping centres in the city, was started by Kristaps Bergs, the real estate king, in the 19th century and has a checkered history. He was one of several children from a farming family in Zemgale and at the age of 16 left to seek his fortune in Riga. The first thing he did was to change his name from Kalnins (small mountain) to Bergs as it was difficult to succeed as a Latvian in a city where most of the businesses were in the hands of the Germans.

He started by buying wooden houses and land just outside the boundaries of the city, and where the hotel Bergs now stands were just cabbage patches.

His main aim was to create a marketplace and over a period he acquired properties piecemeal until he owned a whole block bounded by Dzirnavu in the east, Marijas in the south and Elizabetes in the west. The fact that the the buildings in the centre are of different sizes and heights are due to his changing economic circumstances. "Sometimes, he had money and other times not, so they chart his vicissitudes of fortune," said Ieva Laukers , his great granddaughter who is the custodian of the centre since 1994. Her brother, Justs Karlsons, a lawyer, succeeded in privatising the family properties in 1992. She, working closely with the architect, Zaiga Gaile, has lovingly restored and added new features to the buildings which not only have shops on the ground level but offices on the second and and residences on the third. "It's a village within a city and no cars are allowed," she added proudly.

kalden. The first library was founded in 1524 and the first play, *The Prodigal Son* by a Rigan poet Valdis Burhatds, was performed.

Changing rulers

In 1561, the Livonian Order under its last Grand Master, Gothard Kettler, ceded the country to Poland as they could no longer withstand the Russian attacks and in return Kettler received the Duchy of Courland or Kurzeme (see entry: Rundale). Some twenty years later, the Polish King Stepan Bathory, conquered the city as it had been given an independent status by the previous Grand Master, Walter Plettenberg. Catholicism was reinstated and the Gregorian Calendar introduced that led to Calendar riots in which two of the ringleaders were beheaded. In 1588 the first book was printed in Riga and the Latvian School established in St Jacob's Church.

During the wars between Poland and Sweden, Riga was captured by the Swedish King, Gustavus Adolfus, on September 15th 1621 after a protracted siege that lasted six weeks. Swedish rule which extended for 88 years was termed a golden period because Latvian culture was encouraged, resulting in the publication of the Bible, books and a dictionary in their language. The Bible was translated by a Lutheran Pastor, Ernst Glück, from a grant by the Swedish Administration.

Russian rule

The town was unsuccessfully besieged by Tsar Alexey Mikhailovich in 1656 but the Russians returned in 1709 and the town which had suffered from severe flooding and later, starvation in which two thirds of the inhabitants had died, surrendered on July 4th, 1710 to

Count Sheremetyev. The Count had earlier taken as prisoners Ernst Glück and his family, including his adopted daughter Marta Skrovronska who later married Peter the Great and became Catherine I. The Russian occupation of the town and country was the longest of all foreign powers and continued until 1918.

Nineteenth century – visitors' views

At the beginning of the nineteenth century, a couple of visitors made interesting comments on the city. 'As soon as you drive into Riga,' said Nikolay Karamzin, the Russian historian, 'you will see it as a merchants' city – many shops, many people, the river full of different nations' ships, and the Stock Exchange is so packed, there is no room to turn around'.

Another visitor, BV Peste is, complained about how expensive Riga was, as did Karamzin. He warned other male visitors to be careful when meeting a woman on the street, as it was difficult to distinguish between servants and ladies, because everyone was well dressed. He also wondered at the selection of food which came from all parts of the world. There was wine from Africa, sugar from America, grapes from Astrakhan, port and cheese from England and venison from Poland and Russia.

During the Crimean War the English fleet under Admiral Sir Charles Napier blockaded the town in 1854. In 1857 the fortifications were demolished and reconstruction of the city began which would result in its population increasing sevenfold from some 70,000 to 500,000 by the beginning of the twentieth century.

Riga also became the most important city for science and technology in Russia and the site for the production of railway carriages, cars, aircraft and bicycles.

There was a wave of nationalism that resulted in the formation of the Latvian National Awakening movement launched by Krisjanis Valdemars, Juris Alunans and Krisjanis Barons who in 1862 also founded the 'Newspaper of St Petersburg'. The Baltic Germans, a minority who ran the country saw the newspaper as a threat to their power base and persuaded the Russians to shut it down. In 1868 the Latvian Society was established and in 1873, the first song festival took place in Riga which promoted the development of the Latvian culture.

Twentieth century changes

On January 13th, 1905 there were demonstrations in the city during which seventy people were shot by troops. During the World War I, when Riga was occupied by the Germans, the Russians and the Bolsheviks, and the Latvian Riflemen proved to be a formidable fighting unit, the Latvians saw their first chance of Independence and established the State on November 18th, 1918. On January 26th, 1921 after fighting for Independence for three years Latvia was acknowledged by European nations and admitted to the League of Nations the same year. Over the next two decades many things happened in Riga.

A new currency, the lat, was issued and Janis Cakste was elec-ted the President. The first bus routes and taxis appeared, Radio Latvia started broadcasts and the Ethnographic Museum opened. The Freedom Monument and the Brother's Cemetery were built and the conversion of the five Zeppelin Hangars into the Central Market, the most modern market in Europe, was completed.

The city was relatively prosperous during the two decades between the two World Wars; this was partly due to the authoritarian regime of Prime Minister Karlis Ulmanis who was able to take strong measures in the years of economic depression.

In 1939, due to the secret non-aggression pact between Russia and Germany, the Soviet Union forced upon Latvia a treaty of mutual assistance which amounted to an annexation. Under the Molotov-Ribbentrop agreement all the Baltic Germans left the country. During the World War II, Riga was 'liberated' three times, twice by the Soviets, in 1940 and 1944 and once by the Nazis in 1941. An estimated 600,000 people, a third of the pre-war population perished or disappeared in mass deportations.

The splendid Baroque façade of St Peter's Church

Roof of restored Blackhead's House, with St Peter's Spine in the background

After the war, Riga became multicultural as industrial production was increased and working-men were brought in from all over the Soviet Union.

Independence

The road to the country's Independence began again in the late 1980's. In 1987, on June 14th, protests against the 1941 deportations to Siberia took place at the Freedom Monument. The following year on June 1st, the 1939 Molotov-Ribbentrop agreement was denounced at the Latvian Writers Union Conference. On November 11, the Latvian flag was flown from Riga Castle. On August 23rd 1989, a human chain of over two million Latvians, Estonians and Lithuanians stretched from Tallinn to Riga and Vilnius to protest

Baltic Beach Hotel, Majori, Jurmala

the fiftieth anniversary of the Molotov-Ribbentrop agreement which gave the three republics to the USSR.

A year later, on March 18th, the Latvian Popular Front Party wins elections and on May 4th, the Supreme Council adopted the Declaration of Independence. In 1991, from January 13th to 27th, barricades were set up, outside the house of parliament and around the old town, which were manned twenty-four hours a day. On January 20th, Soviet Special Forces OMON attacked and occupied the Ministry of Interior building and killed seven people. Almost eight months later

Visitors in the nineteenth-century

Independence was again achieved in the twentieth century on August 23rd and ack-nowledged by the USSR on 24th.

On July 8th 1999, the first woman President Vaira Vike-Freiberga was elected. A year earlier, she had been Professor of Psychology at the University of Montreal. 'This is an important hour,' she said in her acceptance speech. 'We open a new page in the history of Latvia.'

Architectural development

Vecriga, the old town, still preserves it Hanseatic features – high storehouses, with spacious granaries and cellars, flanking the narrow winding streets. The only open spaces are the market-place and two other squares.

Medieval times

The medieval Riga was a typical city-state with its rural suburbs which developed close to the city walls around the fourteenth century. The city walls were surrounded by moats, as was the castle, which was outside the walls. There were bastions which were interspersed with ravelins to offer advantage to the city when attacked. (See engraving of M Merian in 1638, Museum of History of Riga and Navigation.)

Until the sixteenth century suburbs around the city were illegal and were frequently destroyed by the Town Council. It was at the behest of the Polish King, Stefan Batory, when the city was ruled by the Polish-Lithuanian alliance, that the first legal suburbs appeared in the 1580s. There was the proviso that the houses were to be built out of timber without cellars and at a sufficient distance from the city walls.

These grew alongside the two main trade routes, the southern towards Russia and the north-eastern along the gulf to Estonia. Few antiquities of the medieval town remain. The oldest church, The Dom (St Mary's) established in 1215, was burned in 1547 and the present building dates from the late 1500s but has been restored since 1883.

St Peter's Church with its beautiful tower 412ft (126m) high was erected in 1406-9. The castle which was built in 1494-1515 by the Master of the Knights of The Livonian Order, Walter von Plettenberg, is a spacious building often rebuilt. The House of the Blackheads, a club of foreign merchants was founded in 1330, and the Dutch renaissance gable was added in 1620. However, it was damaged during the last war and has been restored. The Livlandisch Ritterhaus, a former meeting place for the Livonian nobility no longer exists.

In the sixteenth century the suburbs were inhabited by local peasants and artisans. According to Irena Bakule, The Inspector for Heritage Protection of Riga, a panorama of Riga demonstrates the suburban area sprinkled with farmsteads, one- or two-roomed wooden houses built from horizontal logs with gabled roofs and covered with thatch and scattered alongside roads.

Up to the middle of the nineteenth century, the ancient city of Riga was a fortress enclosed by ramparts, fortified walls and moats. The suburbs had a regular gridiron street layout and blocks divided into large parcels with houses on the streets and orchards with vegetable gardens in the inner area.

Nineteenth-century development

When Napoleon attacked Russia in 1812, the Governor of the city ordered that the suburbs be burned in case of an invasion. It proved to be a false alarm but after the great fire the Russian influence in the rebuilding of the houses was strong and the Classical style for the façades was made compulsory. This regulation also applied to new building in Riga. By the middle of the century, there was rapid development of industry which tended to supplant orchards in the inner space of the blocks and changed the rural character.

As Riga grew the population increased and so did the traffic on the roads out of the Vecriga. There was little space to build new houses or ease the congestion on the roads. The only solution was to expand beyond the city walls as the alternative was untenable, wooden houses in the suburbs which could be burnt down during a siege.

The Town Council approached Governor-General, Prince Alex-ander Suvorov and a petition was taken to St Petersburg. In due course, Tsar Alexander II agreed to give permission for the for-tifications to be pulled down on November 15 1857. A special ceremony was held to mark the occasion in which the Mayor and the Prince were among the first to thrust a spade into the soil. (The spade is still on display in the Riga Museum of History and Navigation.) The demolition work was carried out for the next six years.

Building of the boulevards

A master plan by architects Johann Felsko and Otto Dietze had been approved earlier and the surrounding area was reconstructed according to their plans. The old moat was converted into a canal with gardens and the esplanade was replaced by a semi-circle of boulevards, enclosing the old city, with many public buildings. A large part of the earthworks was carried away and piled up where the sand bastion had stood to create a man-made hill now called Bastion Hill. Coincidentally, a similar process was begun in Vienna when the ramparts that girdled the old town were removed in 1858-60 and replaced by a magnificent boulevard, the Ringstrasse, which was two miles (3.2km) long and lined with trees, splendid buildings and monuments.

New boulevards were formed along both banks of the canal which is now connected with the Daugava River, providing a steady flow. On the old city side, Kronvalda Boulevard, which forms the border of Kronvalda Park, runs first into Basteja and then into Aspazijas Boulevard. The new boulevard on the suburban side has Kalpaka which also borders Krovalda Park and Boulevard Raina runs parallel to Basteja and Aspazijas. (Of course at the time, they were named after the Russian royal family. Street name changes are a common occurrence in the city. From 1919 to 1939, names were changed sixteen times but the record year was in 1923 when 151 streets were renamed). Brivibas or Freedom had previous incarnations as Great Sand, Alexander, Lenin, Revolution and for the shortest period, Adolf Hitler.

The thrust outside the walls and the moats towards the suburbs was a precur-

(cont'd on page 22)

Art Nouveau

To signal the beginning of a new century, Art Nouveau was born. It was a rebellion against eclecticism, that mixture of historical styles, and introduced a contemporary, modern artistic approach based on the concept of turning useful into beautiful. Form follows function. 'Forms emerge from forms and others arise or descend from these. All are related, interwoven, intermeshed, interconnected, interblended... They sway and swirl and mix and drift interminably. They shape, they reform, they dissipate' (Such a description by the US architect Louis Sullivan will suffice to describe this new movement that evolved differently in many countries in the late nineteenth century.)

The 'New Art' movement had a universal appeal. It stimulated linear austerity from Charles Rennie Mackintosh in Glasgow; the steel sinuosities of Victor Horta in Brussels; the chequer-board geometries of Josef Hoffmann in Vienna; Louis Sullivan's vegetal grammar of ornament in Chicago; Antoni Gaudi's eye catching biomorphic surfaces and undulating walls in Barcelona and Mikhail Eisenstein's spectacular operetta of façades in Riga.

The architectural language was characterised as Jugendstil or Youth Style in Germany, Secession in Austria, Eel Style in Belgium and Floral, Noodle or Macaroni Style in Italy, Modernista in Spain and Style Metro in France. But the form of expression was not limited to buildings, it extended to furniture, jewels, paintings, posters, glass, china, clothing, tableware, books, wallpaper and applied arts.

Among the well-known names were Paul Gaugin, Gustav Klint, James Whistler, Henri Toulouse-Lautrec, Edward Munch, Alphonse Mucha and Aubrey Beardsley in painting and posters; Louis Tiffany, Rosenthal, Renee Lalique, Georg Jensen, Liberty and Carlo Bugatti in ornaments and Worth and Paul Poiret in fashion.

In Riga, Art Nouveau found full expression after the city's 700th anniversary exhibition of Industry and Crafts (see The Tale of Two Majors). 'This taste developed especially after the Anniversary Exhibition of 1901, and it was something new indeed' wrote the Latvian art critic Janis Asars at the time.

Opposite: "The Swimmer" by Stafans Bercs (1893-1961). Private collection

Above: Art Nouveau Building

sor to a splendid architectural style that would radically change the city's face from heavy, gloomy Swedish, Germanic and Russian building to the lighter, sophisticated western influences found for example in Paris; hence its nickname in the thirties 'Paris of the North' or 'Little Paris'. However, with the development of the boulevard semicircle came the Eclectic style of stately residences and imposing public buildings; the Opera House, the French Embassy, the National Theatre with its Neo-Renaissance façade, the Riga City Council and the State Museum of Art. It is an outstanding example of town planning in the nineteenth century.

Another important element of the Felsko and Dietze project, was to create green space. The Board of Parks, which was established in 1879, was headed by Georg Kuhfalt who undertook the reconstruction and design of the city's gardens and parks for thirty-five years until 1914. He introduced exotic plants and shrubs and bow-shaped paths, one of which ran behind the National Theatre and is called the Alley of Love.

The twentieth century

At the turn of the century, Riga experienced rapid growth with the population almost doubling to half a million during the course of fifteen years, from 1899 to 1914. Construction now spread far beyond the two bands of semi-circular boulevards towards Tallina Street, en-

Art Nouveau Designer

Mikhail Eisenstein, the father of the Russian film director, was a leading exponent of the eclectic decoration with his amazing designs that combine ornamental motifs from cast cement, ceramics, metal and timber. The top of the frontage of the apartment housed at 2 Alberta Street with its round windows open to the sky is both dramatic and reminds one of the film sets of buildings that were later used by American studios. He was undoubtedly a genius with his designs.

There was little love lost between father and son and Sergei was dismissive and cutting about the buildings. He called him 'a maker of cakes' and urged his friends 'to look at the cream on that house's face'.

'Father, who placed statues of human beings one and a half storeys high, stretched out as a decoration, on the corners of the houses. Father, who deployed women's arms, made from iron drainpipes and with gold rings in their hands, beneath the angle of the roof. In bad weather, it was fun watching the rain stream down between their tin legs. Father, who triumphantly entwined in the sky the tails of the plaster lions – lions de plâtre – which were piled up on the rooftops. Father himself was a lion de plâtre. And he bequeathed to me an unhealthy passion for winding layer upon layer – which I tried to sublimate into a fascination for Catholic Baroque and the over-elaborate work of the Aztecs.'

compassing some eleven streets to the north east. The two-floored wooden models of classicism were replaced by apartment blocks with shops on the ground floor.

The earliest examples of Art Nouveau architecture appeared in Riga in 1899 and were designed by Alfred Aschenkampff for A Grasset's commercial and apartment house at 7 Audeju Street in the heart of the old town *(see page 61)* and Rudolf Zirkwitz's apartment house at 11 Vilandes Street. This should be compared with another building built a year later in Jurmala, 58 Strelnieku Avenue (lit 3) in which similar geometrical designs were used on the walls.

The highlight of any visit to Riga is the Art Nouveau architecture. There are over 200 buildings in the new city and some forty sprinkled in the old town. Although prime examples of the architecture are found in cities like Brussels, Paris, Munich and Vienna, none have such an outstanding collection concentrated in a small area, nor the erotic content eg. 93 Brivibas Street. Many of the houses are in good repair and there are excellent illustrations in Professor Janis Krastins's book, *The Art Nouveau Architecture of Riga*, where he refers to the style as 'music in stone'. I confess that I did not immediately respond to these melodies because I prefer the simpler works of Art Deco. However, after several visits I found the sounds appealing.

Fine façades run along Alberta and Kalku Streets and for aficionados I should mention there are several distinctions of style. Kenins School at 15/17 Terbatas Street illustrates the National Latvian Romanticism that broke out after bloody clashes with Tsarist troops in 1905.

Then there is the perpendicular style of which Janis Gailis's shops and apartment building at 13 Terbatas Street is an example. If you want to take in as many variations of the theme as possible, walk down Smilsu Street. For the record there are seven types including decorative, eclectic, perpendicular, rationalism, national romanticism and gothic revival *(see Walking Tours)*.

A cornucopia of diverse Art Nouveau items other than building can be found in the Riga Museum of History and Navigation *(see separate entry)*.

Business in Riga

Latvia has always been a trading zone between east and west from earliest times, when amber was an important product to barter, to the most recent. The Roman historian Tacitus was complimentary about their diligence as farmers, fishermen and gatherers of glass or amber in the sea, compared to the warlike Germans who showed their characteristic carelessness towards such matters.

Professor Arnis Radins of the History Museum of Latvia mentions that they were good businessmen during the early Iron Age (1AD to 400AD). 'There is evidence that Latvians had trading contacts with all the surrounding territories, particularly the south Baltic', he said. 'They also played a mediator role as many objects from the east and south-west, the Vistula, Niemen and Dnieper, passed through Latvia to Estonia and Finland'.

One of Eisenstein's Masterpieces

Trade

During the Middle Ages, Bremen merchants were the first to visit their settlements and take their products back to Germany and Western Europe. When the Han-seatic towns were formed, Riga became a prominent member. Under the Swedes, it became the largest city in Sweden and later, under the Tsars, it was the second largest commercial city.

According to John Murray's travel handbook in 1865, some 2,000 ships loaded goods: grain, linseed, flax, hemp and wood for export – and imports included salt, herrings, coal, iron, machinery and other goods.

Manufacturing

At the beginning of the twentieth century, Riga was a bustling metropolis and manufacturing industries like the Russian motor industry, textiles, railway carriages and chemicals were located there. Such a position of technological progress was maintained throughout the Soviet era with high-tech industries, e.g. electronics, established in the country.

Banking

One of the youngest top bankers in Central Europe, Valerijs Kargins, would agree that Latvia is now a country of great opportunities. 'There is access to the Soviet economy through acquisitions,' he said.

He is president of Parex Bank, which is the largest in Latvia in terms of assets and capital and controls some twenty-five per cent of the total of core banking services with an authorised capital of $70 million. Together with the

Bank Success Story

Most entrepreneurs are thirtyish and one of the most successful stories concerned Girts Rungainis who built a bank from nothing to the sixth largest, within four years, and although capitalised at $11.8 million, its value rocketed to $40 million after a take-over. After graduating in Latvia, he went to Stockholm University to do a masters degree in banking and finance. There, to make ends meet, he cleaned windows.

On his return he founded the Deutsche-Lettish Bank. In 1995, he obtained the largest loan in the country from the European Bank of Reconstruction and Development and in 1996 achieved another record when his financial transaction was the biggest in Latvia with the sale of the bank to the Hansa Bank.

(cont'd on page 28)

Kemeri station

Tale of two mayors

They stand like bookends at the beginning and end of the twentieth century, George Armitstead and Andris Berzins.

George Armitstead

Mayor from 1901-1912, he got the city off to a head start with a large exhibition to celebrate Riga's 700th year, in the Esplanade, a former parade ground which was turned later into a park. It was an excellent opportunity to demonstrate the city's diverse manufacturing products from ships, cars, railway carriages, motorcycles and bicycles to arts and crafts.

Armitstead came from an interesting background as his grandfather, who was also called George, emigrated from Yorkshire to seek his fortune in the flax business, which was booming in Latvia. He worked at an export company, Mitchel and Co. and later married a local rich girl, Emma von Jakobi. They had six children including John William, George's father.

The family was prominent in Riga. His uncle James was a chairman of the stock exchange and on his death bequeathed the city 500,000 roubles for building and maintaining the first hospital (which still exists today), as well as seventeen paintings from his art collection.

George was the eldest son and after graduating from Riga Polytechnic, the most advanced engineering institute in Russsia, he continued his studies at Zurich and Oxford Universities. In 1874, he married Cecily Pihlau and they had three daughters, one of whom was murdered by the Bolsheviks in 1919.

Before he was appointed Mayor, he was a successful businessman with interests in and outside the city. He founded the Volgunde Brickworks and was a director of both the Baltic Cellulose factory in Sloka and the Dinaburg-Vitebsk railway. In 1888, he chaired the committee of the fourth Baltic Agricultural Exhibition in Riga.

During his term as mayor, he changed the face of the city as most of the two-floor wooden houses were replaced by Art Nouveau buildings, and the Council prohibited the building of new wooden homes. As a result, they now comprise a third of all buildings in the town. The 700th anniversary provided the stimulus as no less than forty pavilions reflected this artisitic style. By the end of 1901 1,172 new projects were approved and it reached a peak in 1910 when approval was given for 1,359. In this area, he has left a lasting monument as the Art Nouveau architecture has been declared a World Heritage Site under UNESCO.

He encouraged the construction of public buildings such as nineteen schools and four hospitals and completed the National Theatre. Public gardens were also a priority and he had nine laid out throughout the city. His crowning achievement, is the creation of the first garden city, Kaiserwald (Tsar's forest now called Mezaparks), north of Riga city and bordering the Kisezers Lake shore.

Essentially there are three divisions in Mezaparks that include the large 1,037-acre (420-hectare) site in which the open-air auditorium is located and where the song festival with 20,000 singers and 40,000 members of the audience are accommodated. The Riga Zoo, which is one of the last projects Armitstead undertook, was opened in 1912 and occupies 59 acres (24 hectares). It is slightly south and just above the residential area, which is another architectural legacy of Armitstead.

The layout of the houses in the Forest Park (Mezaparks) was designed by Georg Kuphaldt, Director of Riga Parks and was begun at the same time as the middle of the city. Art Noveau, National Romanticism, Neo-Classicism and Rationalism are among the styles built in this former pine forest.

He is also credited with opening the first electric tram line (which is still in operation), the covered market and a bridge across the canal on Alexander Street. He was ranked by his contemporaries as the most successful mayor Riga ever had, and Tsar Nicholas II asked him to become Mayor of St Petersburg, a privilege that he declined.

He built himself a castle in the town of Tukums about 45 miles (72km) west of Riga, called Jaunmokas and it is one of the most outstanding examples of red brick style buildings in Latvia. His house can be found on 19 Marstalu Street and another belonging to the Armitstead family is on Nikolaja Street, Riga.

Andris Berzins

He was the mayor who has launched the 800th anniversary of the city initiative, Riga 800, which will be celebrated in 2001. He also has a British connection. He was born in a house in Anglikanu (English) Street opposite the English Seamen's Club (now the Danish Embassy).

The key elements of Riga 800 are humanisation of the city environment through improving transport, building a new bridge across the Daugava, and the creation of a recreation zone. The plan is ambitious as it encompasses the improvement of drinking water and clean air and development of tourism and service industries.

Andris Berzins is a historian and often trips up Swedish visitors with the question 'Which was the biggest city in Sweden during the sixteenth century?' The correct answer is Riga – not Stockholm' as Latvia was part of Sweden at the time. He reminds visitors that Riga of the Thirties was one of the cleanest and most elegant cities in Europe and called Paris of the North or Little Paris.

Although a third of the country's population lives in the city, he managed with only a budget of $340,000,000 a year.

Unibank, the Hansa bank, the Rietumu and Latvijas Krajbanka, it accounts for sixty-one per cent of the sector's assets. They grew through acquiring the oldest Russian bank, the Nobles Livland Bank which was founded in 1782 and local branches of both the Promstroi and MOST banks.

The big break came in 1990, when the reformed but Communist-led Latvian Government, keen to display its independence from Moscow, granted Parex a permit to deal in foreign currency. Kargins and the chairman of Parex, Victor Krasovitsky, opened the first currency exchange office in the USSR. This was a considerable achievement as they were allowed to deal in foreign currency, mainly conversion of the rouble into US dollars. The State had the monopoly in its insatiable quest for hard currency and any other dealings were illegal, and the offenders harshly prosecuted. At the time, the official rate was 60 kopeks to $1 but on the black market the value might have risen to 100 roubles to $1.

Parex developed quickly during perestroika and Latvia's independence, expanding outside its currency exchange operations to become a traditional bank, offering a range of services. Today, the bank is at the top of the official Latvian bank ratings and deals with about thirty per cent of the government's budget.

Victor Krasovitsky believes that the country is no longer a mere link with the East but is an entity in itself through its self-sufficiency policy. 'Latvia has always enjoyed good trading relations with the UK and up to World War II, the UK was its biggest trading partner,' he said. 'Our outlook has always been Western. Latvians have a Western mentality. A new class of business people have developed. They not only have a good education but are willing to devote their life to career building. We are fortunate, as many are employed in this bank.'

Entrepreneurs

Kargins estimates that there are some 100 millionaires in the country and that the BZs (in Latvia entrepreneurs are called the BZs from biezie which means thick wallets) will form a solid core for economic growth. You do not have to look far to see how crowded Riga is with BMWs and Mercedes that have smoked-glass windows. Inside the houses are large fridges, televisions and videos, which is a reminder what Budapest or Warsaw was like when the local entrepreneurs first got going.

The business scene has changed dramatically since Independence when

Beers

Move over Prague and Munich there will soon be another beer capital on the scene. When the rest of Europe discovers Latvian beer, Riga will be put on the map as the place to visit for a fest of real ale.

There are unknown and exotic tastes and aromas to be sampled over a wide range of brands, bottled, on tap and from micro breweries. The beers of great quality are produced by craftsmen and deserve the same consideration as that given to wine. Many visitors in fact rave about these products and drink them instead of wine with their meals. Pale summer ales predominate because most of the beer is drunk during the midsummer festival of Ligo.

The most popular brewery, **Aldaris**, sets the pace because its quality standards are comparable to or even exceed the best in Europe and it still maintains the traditional brewing methods from 1865, when it was established.

An unusual feature of the brewery is that the master brewer is a woman, Inara Sure. She ensures that only natural ingredients are used and recommends connoisseurs to drink Luxus with fish and Zelta with meat. I prefer the Porteris myself, a dark beer which has a high alcohol content of seven per cent. It has a caramel taste with an aroma of wine.

The beer with the most unique taste originates from one of the oldest breweries in the country. Four hundred years old, the Cesis Castle is located in the village of Cesis where the largest beer festival is held every year.

Stalin's preferred beer, Rigas Originalis is pale but with a depth of bitterness that clings to the palate. For those who like lager, (gaisais in Latvian), Bauska is your brand and it is produced by the oldest brewery, so old that there is a folk song about the beer. Other brands worth mentioning include Piebalgas, Tervetes, Dzintars Karla and another strong dark beer, Satans.

Micro breweries are found in every region and the Brenguli is located in a town of the same name about three and a half miles (6km) east of Valmeira. The brewery has its fans who like the bitter which is unfiltered or processed and is described simply as having, 'rich malt aroma and a bitter hop edge'.

people could make a fortune overnight and lose it within a year, according to Girts Rungainis who has now set-up as an investment banker.

'We have good opportunities here', he said, elegantly clad in Yves St Laurent suit in his prestigious offices at 1 Dome Square, 'and excellent human resources as most people are well-educated. My only regret is that we have not yet been

Language

Riga is a cosmopolitan city and although Latvian is the official language, English, Russian and German are widely spoken.

Latvian is an Indo-European language, which belongs to the Balt group like Lithuanian, and has been spoken for a period of 4,000 years. It is closely related to Sanskrit and an interesting link between them for example is the word for water, ava, that is synonymous with Daugava, Latvian for river. For interest it should be noted that all male names end in 's' and female names either 'a' or 'e'.

discovered by the key members of the European Union like the UK, Germany and France. We are only known by Northern Europe'.

Another remarkable entrepreneur, who is already using western marketing methods – an unusual feature in the business world, to grow his television company is Andrejs Ekis. He is full of Murdoch quotes such as 'Think global, be local' and I am sure if the media tycoon came to hear of him, he would snap him up and get him to establish an empire in Russia and Eastern Europe. 'I started with an idea to create breakfast television' he said, 'and then I bought a company that transmitted the evening news. Next I filled the space in between and had the first and only independent TV station in the country'.

Again only thirtyish, he is now the biggest player in the market and reaches eighty-six per cent of the Latvian population. He appreciates that Riga is a cosmopolitan city, the largest in northern Europe and although the country, with its 2.5 million population, is small there are terrific opportunities, particularly if one uses the country as a stepping-stone to the vast Russian market.

'We have all the facilities in this country to launch products into the CIS' he said. 'We can use top Russian actors and have a measure of their psychology. The biggest mistake westerners make is to deal directly with them. The Russians consider a western businessman as a duck they can hunt. There are countless stories of how money disappears and no one knows where'. He admits that there are problems with bureaucracy but points out that you can always find a reasonable official.

Food, cuisine and drink

There is a world of difference between food and cuisine and both are obtainable in Riga. The food is similar to other northern European destinations, heavy and solid, which is well suited to the climate.

Latvian specialties

However, there are surprises in their specialties, soups galore for both summer and winter: beetroot or borsch and sour cream barley soup (skaba putra) served cold for hot weather; for below zero temperatures there is cabbage soup or dried pea and bacon soup which is so thick that it can be described as a stew and is considered to be a national dish. Another unusual soup is a milk fish soup called zivjupiena.

Main courses include simply adding meatballs to the soups, pork in aspic which has accompaniments of mustard or horseradish, potato pancakes served with sour cream and a wide range of smoked meat and fish, particularly sprats for which the region is famous. Piragi, a pastry filled with bacon or other meat and onions is popular and no celebration is complete without it.

Desserts recommended are the Alexander torte, raspberry or cranberry filled pastry strips and a bread pudding or Rupjmaizins pudins made with black or rye bread which is as light and tasty as any French patisserie.

The Central Market

For a quick introduction to Latvian food you can do no better than go to the Central Market next to the Railway Station. Les Halles and Covent Garden have disappeared and it is refreshing to find this remarkable landmark still intact. 'It's a unique experience to visit these vast halls that housed airships', said Oliver Staas, General Manager at Radisson SAS Hotel. 'The buildings are still in good condition. I go once a week with my chef as the quality of food is outstanding.' Each Zeppelin hangar exclusively sells either meat, fish, dairy products or fruit and vegetables. The market is open daily from 8am to 5pm. On Sundays it closes at 3pm.

Top restaurateurs

With cuisine the territory in Riga is divided into two areas, Vincents and Zagars; the celebrity chef versus the latter-day Conran. If you come to Latvia you have to try either one or both.

Martins Ritins

Martins Ritins, who runs Vincents in its various forms from official event catering, the restaurant, and teaching students to the celebrity chef weekly television show, is British, born of Latvian parents who left during the last war. He returned to the country in 1992 after working as a cook in Canada, Saudi Arabia and Jamaica. There were no private restaurants at the time and he opened the first, Vincents, which is named after the famous artist. 'When I arrived there were only canteens to eat in', he said. 'Institutionalised cooking in fact reigned supreme'.

He recalled that when he introduced leaf salads to his menus, many customers sent the food back to the kitchen.Their message was, 'This is food for rabbits, where's the potatoes and meat?'

The food scene is slowly changing and Rigans are coming round to healthier eating. He is a pioneer and besides influencing people's palates, he is encouraging farmers to grow healthier grains or breed quality stock. An inveterate foodie, he raves about a bottle of aromatic extra virgin olive oil and the wild mushrooms he can buy for only £1.50 a kilo rather than £40 a kilo in the UK.

His appreciative clients include ambassadors and celebrities like B B King, Rostropovitch, José Carreras and the British Royal family. Both Prince Charles and Prince Andrew came to dine. During the summer if you sit on the terrace you can enjoy Charolais beef steak, guinea fowl or sushi and watch the in-crowd of the city.

Lido

Gunars Kirsons, president of Lido is the leading exponent of traditional Latvian food and his restaurants are found all over the city. For visitors, it is worthwhile a visit as they will be surprised at the moderate prices and the excellent quality of the cuisine.

1. Walking Tours

Walking is one of the best ways to get the feel of a city and Riga is no exception. Two walks are described here, the first exploring Vecriga and the second looking at the wonderful Art Nouveau architecture to be found here.

Tour One: Old Riga or Vecriga

The tour begins at the **Gunpowder Tower**, a striking red brick building with dolomite foundations, which is located at the intersection of **Smilsu** and **Torna Streets**. The tower, which was built at the beginning of the fourteenth century is part of the medieval wall. It is the only one of the twenty-five towers left and was in use until the sixteenth century. The distance between each tower was determined by the range of an arrow, which was

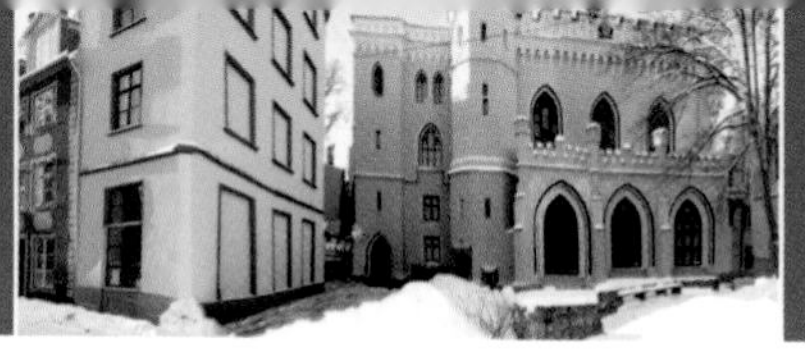

Opposite page: Dom Church

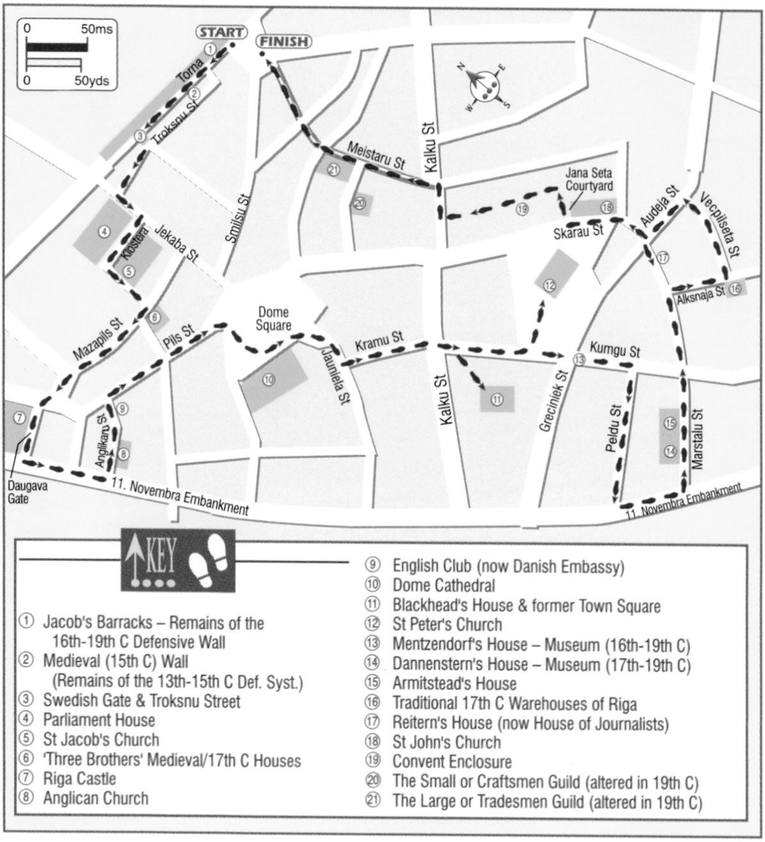
0 50ms
0 50yds
START
FINISH
Torna
Troksnu St
Jekaba St
Klostera
Smilsu St
Meistaru St
Kalku St
Jana Seta Courtyard
Skarau St
Audeja St
Vecpilseta St
Alksnaja St
Dome Square
Mazapils St
Pils St
Kramu St
Jauniela St
Kumgu St
Greciniek St
Peldu St
Marstalu St
Anglikanu St
Daugava Gate
11. Novembra Embankment
KEY
① Jacob's Barracks – Remains of the 16th-19th C Defensive Wall
② Medieval (15th C) Wall (Remains of the 13th-15th C Def. Syst.)
③ Swedish Gate & Troksnu Street
④ Parliament House
⑤ St Jacob's Church
⑥ 'Three Brothers' Medieval/17th C Houses
⑦ Riga Castle
⑧ Anglican Church
⑨ English Club (now Danish Embassy)
⑩ Dome Cathedral
⑪ Blackhead's House & former Town Square
⑫ St Peter's Church
⑬ Mentzendorf's House – Museum (16th-19th C)
⑭ Dannenstern's House – Museum (17th-19th C)
⑮ Armitstead's House
⑯ Traditional 17th C Warehouses of Riga
⑰ Reitern's House (now House of Journalists)
⑱ St John's Church
⑲ Convent Enclosure
⑳ The Small or Craftsmen Guild (altered in 19th C)
㉑ The Large or Tradesmen Guild (altered in 19th C)

around 22ft (7m). It acquired its name during the Swedish period when gunpowder was stored there and to ensure durability, three horse heads have been immured in the 1ft (31cm) thick tower walls.

Another name for the building was Smilsu or Sand tower because the city was surrounded by sand hills and the tower also served as a main entrance to the city because a gatehouse was placed next to it. Relics of earlier periods can be seen including rings for securing cannons in the windows, the thick walls that could withstand the impact of cannon balls (nine Russian balls are embedded in the walls) and a vaulted chamber which was the assembly point for the soldiers. (This is where the café is now located). There are good views from the tower of the old town.

The **Latvian War Museum** is housed in the tower and is devoted to military history, particularly featuring exhibits that depict the country's struggle for independence. Of special interest is the Latvian Riflemen or Strelnieks, both white and red, whose exploits were so remarkable that they served as Lenin's special guards in the Kremlin.

Walk down Torna Street and on the right is **Jacob's Barracks**, which runs the whole length of the street. The building with basements is the longest in the city and was built in the eighteenth century. On the left are the restored remnants of the city wall (thirteenth to fifteenth century) which included the small rectangular Ramer's tower.

Further along are several private houses and at Number Eleven you will find the **Swedish Gate** which was built in 1698 when Riga was part of Sweden and its largest city. It was one of the eight gates of the defending wall and was opened at sunrise and closed at sunset. Inside the building, which is now the **House of Latvian Architects**, extending from the basement to the first floor are the remains of another tower, the Jirgens.

It is traditional for newly weds to walk through the Swedish Gate to ensure a happy life. The house was the first to be owned privately in the city and was bought in 1679 by Ivan Serpentin. Two rooms in the house are open to the public.

Walk through the Swedish Gate and turn right into Troksnu or Alarm Street. This is a vestige of the inner side of the defending wall, where townsmen had to congregate to defend the city against attackers. Notice the uneven cobbles which resulted from a regulation that required the citizens to maintain the street by supplying cobble stones. Each craft had to be responsible for a sector and had to equip their members with armaments and six leather buckets.

At the end of the street you will face **The Saeima or Parliament Building**, which was originally, the Vidzeme Knight's House or House of the Nobles. It was reconstructed in 1867 in the style of a Florentine Renaissance Palace by prominent Latvian architects Janis F Baumanis and Robert Pflug. After the Agrarian reforms in 1920, it became the Latvian parliament.

Turn left in Jacob Street and follow the building round into Klostera or Monastery Street. There you will find one of the three important landmarks of the city which appeared on medieval maps and provided the famous view: **St Jacob's Cathedral**. The cathedral was build in 1225 for people in the suburbs and the poor to worship as it was then located outside the city wall, (the rich had the Dome) and is the only church which still has a Gothic spire. It has a

Ghostly cries

Again there is a tale of an immurement or rather two tales. A Latvian girl fell in love with a Swedish soldier and wanted to marry him. Such a relationship was forbidden and she was caught and entombed alive in the wall. Another variation also concerns a young girl who tried to escape the city during the black plague but was caught and given the same treatment. Whichever story is true, her cries can be heard on New Year's Eve.

unique feature on the southern side, a bell that hung under a protective cupola outside the spire. If you look up you will still be able to see the cupola as the 'balcony bell' has long since been removed.

The bell was also called the 'wretched sinner's bell' as one of the uses was to announce that a hanging would take place in the Town Hall square. (The last hangman, incidentally, lived at 9 Torna Street and the occupation was hereditary). Another meaning associated with the bell was that it would automatically ring whenever an unfaithful wife passed below. There was a period when it rang continually and this so upset the townspeople that it was taken down and thrown into the Daugava. The bell has never been replaced.

As a cathedral it has a rather austere basilica interior and as you enter, inscribed on the portal is *Misericordias domini in aeternum cantabo*, translated as 'Sing the Lord's mercy forever'. It is white inside with brickwork that outlines the different shapes such as the vaulted ceiling, arches and windows. The altar is simple and the cathedral has a choir room, a parish hall and a 27ft (8m) tall steeple.

There is evidence of two entombments in the cathedral. In the northern wall a niche was found to contain a man's skeleton with his clothes which were well preserved and showed that the person was from the upper classes. The other entombment was of a man called Indrikis and is described in documents at the city archives. He wanted to be worshipped in this life and the next and there-fore wanted to be buried alive in the walls. The Brothers of the Franciscan monastery who had jurisdiction of the cathedral agreed to his request.

The building is an amalgam of different periods. The main part dates back to the thirteenth century, the cupola for the outside bell was added during the fifteenth century, the lower part of the octagonal tower two centuries later and its roof pyramid in 1756.

Changes of allegiance

The cathedral has a mixed religious history. First it was for Catholics and during the Reformation its status changed and it became the first church to hold a Lutheran service in 1522. When the Polish King Stepan Bathory conquered the city in 1582, it was handed over to the Jesuits. In 1621, when the Swedes arrived, St Jacobs became a garrison church. For the next three centuries it remained in the Protestant camp until the twentieth century when it reverted to Catholicism.

Opposite the cathedral is the eighteenth-century **church of Mary Magdalene** that was also once a convent. Walk down the street towards Maza Pils or Small Castle Street which when you turn right leads to Riga Castle.

Facing you are **'The Three Brothers'** at No.'s 17, 19 and 21, which are outstanding medieval architectural monuments. The nick-name derives from the fact that they represent

The Small Guild in Meistaru Street

residential buildings from the fifteenth, sixteenth and seventeenth century respectively which are adjacent. Each house has a gable, the simplest design is No.17, which ascends in three steps with Gothic niches, slightly askew and is the oldest stone house in the city.

It is also the furthest from the street as the space in front was used as a porch for benches and beside the door are two large identity stones. A clue to the former owner is given by the coat of arms that includes ears of wheat. It belonged to a baker and was the site of the first pastry shop. The other two are closer to the street as space was at a premium and additional floors were added.

The **Museum of Architecture** is housed in No.19 and it is worth a visit to get an impression of the inside of this sixteenth-century building. Examples of models, plans and sketches of Johann Felsko, Janis Baumanis and others can also be seen. The building, which was renovated in 1646, has an interior also from the same period including a fireplace.

All the Brothers had similar interior layouts as the ground and first floors were used for living space for the family and servants, while the upper floors including the attic, were used for storage. Hatches were placed in the middle of the ceiling to move goods up and down on a system of pulleys.

Sometimes access was also gained by placing beams outside the building for lifting big and heavy objects into attic storage rooms.

Riga Castle is found at the end of the street which becomes the Castle Square or Pils Laukums. The present castle building, originally square-shaped with four towers including two rounded ones, was built in 1515 by the townsmen. They had already destroyed three earlier buildings of the Brothers of the Sword and the Livonian Order who decided it was safer to be outside the city walls.

During the Swedish and Russian periods an additional wing was added on the northern side including a polygonal bay window tower which had limestone carvings of animals, men and gargoyles. The reliefs, splendid examples of seventeenth-century decorative art, can be seen if you walk round it. A fifth tower, designed by Eizens Laube, the three-star tower of national unity was added in 1938.

The castle is the residence of the President of Latvia, Vaira Vike-Freiberga, and also contains magnificent reception halls. She has her own orchestra, the Latvian army band which plays on ceremonial occasions. Whenever she is at home, the special Presidential flag flies from the Holy Ghost Tower which served as part of the city's fortifications and is opposite the Lead Tower with

Top Ten Architectural Styles

A list of the top ten buildings in Riga which should not be missed by anyone with an interest in architecture, has been compiled with the co-operation of Irena Bakule of the Latvian State Inspection for Heritage Protection.

1. Art Nouveau buildings in The Old Town, the following streets have three or more buildings: Kalku, Smilsu, Marstalu, Skunu, Valnu and Alberta Street.
2. St Peter's Church with viewing platform.
3. Dome Cathedral and its organ.
4. Mentzendorff House Museum corner of Grecinieku and Kungu Streets (opposite).
5. Reutern House, 2 Marstalu Street.
6. Kemeri Hotel, Kemeri and Hotel Majori, Majori (see page 67).
7. St Saviours Anglican Church in Anglikanu Street.
8. Ethnographic Open-air Museum, 440 Brivibas Street, just outside city limits.
9. Jacob's barracks in Torna Street.
10. Konventa Seta complex between Kaleju and Skarnu Streets which includes oldest building, St George's Church.

its conical roof. The Castle also houses three museums, the **Museum of Foreign Art**, the **Museum of Latvian History** and the **Rainis Museum of Literature and Art**.

As you leave the Castle head for the river down **Daugava Gate**. Turn left into the **11th November Embankment** which, was the site of the Daugavmala or Daugava's edge market for almost four centuries, and again take the second left into Anglikanu or Anglican Street. This is named after the **Factory Church of St Saviour of Riga** and was built by British merchants in 1859.

Over two thousand English ships visited Riga every year during the eighteenth century and religious services were shared with German and Dutch sailors and merchants in the Reformation Church in Marstalu Street. The arrangement was unsatisfactory as they were conducted in German.

Another bit of Britain was built at the end of the street, a club for English Officers, some forty years later. As you pass you can notice three reliefs above the window of the balcony, a shamrock, a rose and a thistle. Each are symbols for Ireland, England and Scotland respectively.

The club, now the **Danish Embassy**, was designed by the well-known Latvian architect Wilhelm Bockslaff who also has several other fine buildings to his credit including Art Nouveau style at 25 Jauniela and 6 Kalku Streets,

Hated citizen

The last Grand Master of the Livonian Order, Walter von Plettenberg, added his sculptural relief to the patroness of the Order, St Mary and both were placed above the gate. He was held in such odium by citizens that he eventually left Riga and spent his last years in Cesis.

Armitstead's Jaunmokas Castle and the red brick Latvian Academy of Art. The richest merchants in Riga were the British whose influence lasted until World War II. During the 1890s, half the export trade of Latvia was with the UK.

We now turn right into Pils or Castle Street and head for the heart of Old Riga, the **Dome Square**. **The Dome**, which originates from Domus Dei (The House of God) was the seat of Bishop Albert and one of the three powers in the city sharing influence with the Town Hall and Livonian Order. Bishop Albert consecrated an ancient burial ground of the original inhabitants, the Curonians or the Cours, in 1211 and started to build the church which would later become the largest in The Baltics. It is a superb artistic and architectural landmark and has dominated the city's skyline for almost seven centuries.

At a lower elevation than other buildings it was a victim of floods during 1709 and an embankment was built on Jauniela Street to prevent inundation in the future. The original foundation marks the original level of Riga and shows how the debris was built up over the centuries, giving the wrong impression that subsidence has occurred. The thirteenth-century Gothic portal, formerly the main entrance, appears now to be buried. To gain entry to the northern portal one has to descend sixteen steps. It was built on the cross but this has been obscured through multiple additions during various periods.

The church's oldest sections, the altar alcove and east wing crossing, are excellent examples of the early Romanesque-style with its high walls, rows of semi-circular windows and crosswise vaulted ceiling. The Gothic style extensions are distinguished by their simplicity – pointed arches, stellar vaults and large windows. The eastern pediment and the steeple were reconstructed in 1776 in the Baroque manner.

The portal was refashioned by

(cont'd on page 42)

English Church

Representatives of the English Trading Company gained permission from the Tsar to erect their own church. The Neo-Gothic building, a classic example of the Eclectic style was designed by Johann Daniel Felsko and was built on English soil which was part of the foundation. The bricks too came from England and were brought as ballast in ships. The cost of the project came to some 86,000 roubles. The Church was conveniently situated near the river and enabled English ships to dock not far away so that the sailors and merchants could attend services before going about their business.

Tour of the Dome

Enter the church from the western portal and turn left into St Mary's Chapel. The old altar was once installed here and because it was low the view of the new stained glass windows was not obscured but it disappeared when concerts were held.

We move towards the northern side and the Tiesenhausen Chapel which was dedicated to one of the oldest families in the Baltic states. The Tiesenhausens donated two stained glass windows in 1883, one of which depicts the family with the Virgin Mary and angels and the other is of Bishop Albert with the builder of the Dome. The epitaph and grave plaque of an earlier ancestor, Mary Tiesenhausen, who died in 1611, is attached to the wall.

There are two further stained glass windows in the next chapel which show historical events of 1525 and 1621 respectively. The Grand Master of the Livonian Order, Walter von Plettenberg, read his edict on religious freedom in the Town Square and vowed to protect the citizens from the Catholic Archbishop's claim to restore Catholicism. The Swedish King, Gustavus Adolfus, in his moment of triumph was welcomed by the Mayor of Riga, Herman Samson and the Town Councillors in front of the Dome after he had conquered the city. They were pleased with the King as he had liberated them from the yoke of Catholic Poland.

At the northern wing crossing, there are stained glass side windows designed by the local artist Ernst Tode in 1902 who also provided the Art Nouveau-style stained glass windows at the Latvian Academy of Art. Two windows describe the lives of St Martin and St George, while the third, which was made in the Urbana workshops in Dresden, depict the Apostles Peter and Paul.

There is a memorial at the crossing, of the notorious mayor Nicolas Ecke, who appears to have embezzled funds while he was the city's treasurer. He was so reviled by the citizens that he was thrown out of the city on two occasions. Before his death however, he tried to make amends through the establishment of a home for six or more old, poor widows at 22 Skarnu Street, the Ecke's Convent. To assuage their fury, he had inscribed on the façade, the words, 'The aim of my life is Christ', which was placed above a relief of Christ and The Sinner, implying, 'Let him who is without sin throw the first stone'. All this was to no avail as an alabaster head of him, which adorned the memorial, was broken off. It was replaced in the last century.

At the altar niche are three stained glass windows which were made at the Weber and Kalerta workshops, with an image of Christ in the middle, a scene from the Old Testament on the left and on the right one from the New Testament. Along the wall is an exciting find, two long benches, which date from pre-Reformation days, with fine carvings on both. There is a picture of Adam and Eve in the Garden of Eden on one and of Mary Magdalene on the other.

The only grave in the Dome is found here in the left wall. It is of Bishop Meinhard who built the first stone and brick church at Ikskile, south of Riga on the Daugava River. He died in 1196 and his remains were brought to the Dome for burial in the fourteenth century.

At the crossing of the south wing, we find further stained glass windows depicting scenes from both the Old and New Testament. On the wall is a plaque denoting the water level during the 1709 flood.

Aerial view of the Dome and Dome Square

In the central area we can see the magnificent organ and the memorable pulpit which both feature fine woodwork. The pulpit, which was gifted to the church in 1641, was supposedly designed and carved by Tobias Heinz, the artist from Jelgava, and the angel was sculptured by Imhof in 1817. The pews, ornamented with black heads, are for the Society's members (see Blackhead's House).

The organ, which has always been considered as the Dome's greatest treasure, has 6718 pipes with 124 pitches, two consoles with four manuals and a pediclavier. When it was completed and installed in 1884 by Walcker Ludvigsburg, it was the largest in the world.

The original organ was designed by Jakob Raabs in 1601 in the Mannerism style and embellished with Baroque and Rococo motifs in the seventeenth and eighteenth century. The woodwork was decorated with fantastic animals, angels and wreaths of flowers.

Weather vanes

On the south side the golden cock can be seen and the windows which sported stained glass that were destroyed during the war are bricked in. The original weathercock was two-sided, a gold and a black side. When ships saw the black cock, it represented bad weather and there would be no entry into the port. Before you head towards Kramu or Garbage Street go to the middle of the square and you can see the three golden weather cocks on St Peter's, the Dome and St Jacob's.

Johann Felsko in 1862 and the new Art Nouveau vestibule was completed at the turn of the last century. Although the architectural features inside highlight its grandeur, the highly decorative interiors were lost during the Reformation and what was left was mostly removed during Soviet times when the church was converted into a concert hall in 1960.

Outside in the huge Dome square you can comprend why everyone usually ends up there as seven streets converge on the square and cafés as well as street markets are popular in the area.

Pass along Kramu Street, across Kalku and veer right where you will find the former Town Hall Square and the most splendid building in the city. There, the **Blackheads' House**, or Melngalvju, was a society of unmarried, rich foreign merchants that originated in the thirteenth century, initially under the patronage of St Mauritius. He was a black martyr who had been a tribune in a Roman Legion and the coat of arms consisted of an oval gold frame surrounding a black turbaned head, a sword and a cross against a red background. Later there were other patrons including St George and St Gertrude.

The building, which is being restored, was first mentioned in 1334 when it housed part of the Riga Guild, and it was only later in 1477 that it became associated with the Blackheads, through their rental of the upper floors. They acquired the building in 1713.

A unique feature of the house is the vast ornate gable which was derived from Dutch influences. Adrian and Lambert Jensen supervised the rich ornamentation that included crowning the stepped gable with sculptures of people such as St George and St Gertrude, animals and obelisks. The steps of the gable were decorated with intertwined ribbons, and spirals carved in stone. The six inches (15cm) of the pediment had paintings of deities like Mercury and Neptune, and a tower clock with an 'eternal clock calendar' showing the month, day, hour, minute and phase of the moon, was placed above the central niches in 1622. A relief bust of King Arthur too was included in a shallow niche, as both the King and his Knights of the Round Table were an integral part of their social activities.

The top of the gable was crowned by a remarkable feature, three metallic poles. The central pole, which was the longest and made of gilded copper, carried the remarkable weathercock representing St George and the Dragon, with a sword in his hand. It weighed some 66lbs (30 kg) and was made by the Riga jewel maker Eberhard Meyer in 1622.

Through its regulations, the society resembles a British Club and one would imagine that women, married or otherwise, would have been barred as no married men could be members. Card and dice games were prohibited as well as carrying swords into the premises.There was no doubt as to who was welcome there as there was a stricture that did not allow soldiers or craftsmen entry, as it was for officers only, starting with ensigns. The members actively participated in social life, founded schools and established charities. They had balls at which women were welcome, as on an occasion in 1762 when Catherine II arrived incognito and joined in the dancing.

Opposite the Blackheads, is **St Peter's Church** which has always been a familiar landmark because it was the tallest building in the city. It has always been the stronghold of the citizens and Town Council and was the base of their power in the city. Built in the thirteenth century, it was mentioned in a chronicle in 1297 when citizens bombarded the castle with stones from its tower during clashes with the Livonian Order of Knights.

Some believe that the church is the most beautiful in Riga because of the symmetrical shape and the spire which is a masterpiece of fusion of Gothic and Baroque styles. But the spire has had its share of bad luck with several fires and when it was struck by lightening Peter the Great was on hand and helped to prevent the fire from spreading to nearby houses. (The Tsar lived in the city for a period and his castle is found at 9 Palace Street).The last spire fortunately lasted the longest from 1746 to 1940, some 195 years. Sadly little has survived from its past glory when the church was burnt down in 1941 and rebuilt in 1984.

There are two viewing platforms in the belfry which enable visitors to see the panorama of the city as well as the sea on a clear day. We leave the church and move in the direction of The Blackheads House before turning left towards the corner of Grecinieku or Sinners and Kungu or Masters' Streets where the wealthy merchant Mentzendorff's house is located *(see page 48).*

The seventeenth century was a prosperous period for Riga because of the great demand in western Europe for timber, flax, hemp and grain from the East. Riga served as the point of transhipment at a time when Russia had no access to the Baltic and the trade enriched merchants in the city.

For a glimpse of the sort of people involved look no further than a painting by an unknown artist which hangs in the **Museum of the History of Riga and Navigation**. A group of men in dark garments with broad collars sit on high chairs round a table covered with black cloth. Each person has a pile of money in front of him and they share a large silver mug of beer and a goblet of wine. Such profitable trade stimulated shipbuilding as well as the construction of magnificent many floored houses with attics on four to five floors for storage *(see page 36).*

(cont'd on page 46)

'The amazing thing about the city is that everything can be found within walking distance'

Sandra Inlkena of Riga Tourism

For future information:

Riga Dome City Council, Valdemara iela 3, Riga LV-1539, Latvia
Phone: +371 702 6177. Fax: +371 702 6337

Once in Kungu Street note the cupola at the top of the house on the Grecinieku side where pulleys would be operated. Cupolas are found in most medieval houses. Walk down Kungu and turn first right into Peldu or Swim Street in the direction of the Daugava and turn left into the 11th November Embankment and left again into Marstalu Street.

Dannenstern House at No.21 is an excellent example of Baroque architecture with an unusual feature of glazed roof tiles. It was owned by Ernst Metsue, a self-made man of Dutch origin who started off as a tradesman and ended up with a fleet of vessels. He was rich enough to build, in 1696, the largest private house in Riga. On the way up he acquired the title of von Dannenstern. The façade is decorated with eight pilasters crowned with elegant capitals. Stone heads of fantastic animals are on the right and left side of the roof and the two entrances are richly decorated with stone carvings. A Swedish sculptor, D Walter and a Swiss stonemason created the magnificent façade.

A large hall, an office and the business quarters were on the ground floor. The family rooms are spread over two floors, the first and the second. The vast attic was used as a storeroom and goods were also stored in the basements.

Marstalu or Mary's Stable Street is worth lingering in, as there are several other interesting buildings. Next door at No.19 is where George Armitstead, a former mayor, lived *(see entry, Tale of Two Mayors)*. Move up the street towards Audeja or Weaver Street. On the right, you can spot a steeple that will indicate the **Reformed Church**, at the corner of Alksnaja or Alder Grove Street, and one of the few Calvinist places of worship.

The church was built by Kristofers Meinert, who was the grandfather of the famous Latvian architect Kristofers Haberland. The latter was responsible for many houses in Riga in the Classical style which had the singular features of façades decorated with columns on either side of the door and a central window with balcony above on the first floor. They were built of bricks with flat ceilings and only basements were vaulted *(see No.5 Smilsu Street)*. It is the only Baroque church in the city and in a break with tradition, has a star rather than a cock as a weathervane. The upper part of the façade is crowned with a cupola and open gallery, a design more common in northern Europe than the Baltics.

When it was rebuilt after a fire in 1805, the first floor was lifted and storerooms created under it. These spaces have now been turned into a concert hall and restaurant respectively.

We will first go down **Alksnaja** to see a traditional seventeenth-century warehouse before returning to the top of Marstalu Street. As trade boomed, the attic storerooms became insufficient and purpose-built storehouses were constructed. They were large brick or stone buildings with tiled roofs and their butt-ends faced the street, such as No's.7, 8, 10 and 11 which remains entirely unchanged.

The roof rested on a row of strong beams that ran the width of the building. The doors were usually made of oakwood and a stone emblem, representing a bird, animal or strange beast was placed above the door or next to it. Sometimes the animal would be simply painted on a wall.

Under the roof of the warehouse in the courtyard was a special device for lifting goods. It was a windlass fastened to a beam and men would pull the rope tied to the goods up or down to the desired floor. In some instances there was a tower with a spiral staircase that led up to the windlass such as No.11.

During the eighteenth century there were about 160 warehouses in the city and some ten can still be found on Vecpilsetas Street. If you wish to see the inside of an old warehouse, the one at 3 Vecpilsetas has been transformed into a restaurant called The Big Camel.

We move round the corner to the beginning of Marstalu Street where we find another seventeenth-century building, **Reutern House**, that belonged to John Reutern, another Dutch merchant of the same name. It was designed by Rupert Bindenschuh, who set a trend by abandoning the gabled style and adopting Baroque. Instead he used Corinthian columns and portraits of the owners of the house above them. The façade is also decorated with a group of sculptures depicting a battle between a bear and lion that represented the Northern War at the beginning of the eighteenth century between Sweden and Russia.

Of particular beauty are the stone garlands over the first floor windows and running along the upper part of the building, above the six pilasters, is a stone frieze representing animals alternating with leaves and flowers. The splendid façade has been preserved for over three centuries while the interior was refurbished several times. It is now the Journalists' House.

We are now off to see the fourth and last church and head left towards Skarnu or Butcher's Street, which was the site of the former meat market. There is a connection between **St John's Church** and Reutern House as the architect, Rupert Bindershuh, who died in 1698, is buried there.

The church and a cloister was built by the Dominican friars in the thirteenth century when Bishop Nicholas gave them the former Bishop's palace, which was built by Bishop Albert. In 1500 the church was rebuilt after a fire and except for the monastery gates and north-west entrance everything was new. A high-stepped pediment was built above the north-west wall, its vertical stripes of red brick alternate with lightly-hued plaster work.

Life-size, sandstone statues of John the Baptist in prison and Salome carrying his head are installed in niches on the wall in Jana or John Street, where the first Riga castle occupied by Bishop Albert was situated. Distinctive features inside are the net vaults, its Baroque altar, the August Stilling altar pieces and stained glass windows. The painting by Janis Rozentals called *The Crucified* is in the Sacristy *(see page 99)*.

We now enter Jana Seta or John's courtyard, a narrow passage between the church and Ecke's Convent. The cloister gate with its Gothic frame, has embellishment or arc known as 'The Donkey's Back' and is a vestige from the original thirteenth-century building. The arc is repeated on St John's pediment.

Wealthy Merchants' houses

Mentzendorff's House and Dannenstern's House are excellent examples of the above. The former was built in 1695 by Jurgen Helm, a Town Councillor, and was bought in 1884 by the wealthy merchant August Mentzendorff whose descendants lived here until the last war.

For over 200 years it has had a dual use as a family home and a pharmacy owned by the Briedis's. A fascinating interior belies the plain, austere exterior and the museum, an affiliate of the Museum of History of Riga and Navigation, is worth a visit. It has been furnished and decorated with authentic pieces from the seventeenth and eighteenth centuries, and gives the visitor a good impression of life during those periods.

On the ground floor, there is an open fireplace with copper and tin kitchen utensils and the laboratory and shop, with a rare cash collegiate desk. Each floor surprises: there is a Watteau room where the walls are painted with motifs from Antoine Watteau works; a small family chapel; a Bohemian room of a young poet; a living room with an old piano, old masters on the wall and a card-desk with an ancient deck of cards; and the big entrance hall with the clay floor.

There is an interesting display of products in the chemist shop including Riga's Black Balsam. Its healing qualities were attributed mainly to its application to wounds, stings, tumours and fractured bones. Little thought was given to quaffing it. The museum is open 10am to 5pm, Wednesday to Sunday, ☎ 721 2951 and ☎ 722 2636.

Next to John's courtyard is another courtyard called **Konventa Seta** or Convent Courtyard, which is now a complex of a hotel, shops, art galleries and cafés and is one of the most beautiful in the city. As you pass through you can see the old city walls on one side and a relief of the Riga coat of arms.

In the restoration of the wall, it was found that grout mixed with dolomite stones was used for the foundation which was laid on sand. The wall itself was built of limestone and faced with bricks. Inside the fortifications, it consisted of two tiers, the lower one in peacetime could be used for storing goods and providing shelter for the homeless. In the Jana Seta the upper part of the wall, the passage, was supported by arches and covered by a wooden roof with tiles. The defenders of the city would stand there and peer through the loopholes at the enemy before they hurled the spears or fired at them with arrows or bullets.

The total height of the wall was about 36ft (11m) and its thickness 8ft (2.5m) at the basement. Whenever the city was in danger various crafts and guilds participated in its preservation, each manning a tower or specific area of the wall.

Konventa Seta was derived from the Holy Spirit Convent which moved here when the first Riga Castle, which had occupied the land, had been destroyed and a new castle had been built on the convent's former site near the river.

The Grey Sisters, an order of Franciscan nuns with a grey habit, took care of the sick, looked after invalids and an additional duty was to educate children. They also had a rule which enabled them to leave the order whenever they chose. The symbol for the Holy Spirit is a dove or pigeon and later, when the

Architecture

buildings were used as warehouses, the bird was adopted by their owners. Consequently, reliefs of doves in different hues were engraved on the buildings.

The courtyard contains a ruin from the old stone structure of the first castle built in 1204 which is now part of the interior of the Hotel Konventa Seta. Fragments of the chapel and assembly hall survived the fire that destroyed it and can be seen in St George's Church which is now part of the Museum of Applied and Decorative Art. It was divided up into three storage areas, the white, the blue and the brown dove and used as such until 1986.

Exit from Konventa Seta in Kalku Street and turn right towards **Philharmonia Square**. When you reach it turn left in Meistaru or Masters' Street. There you will find the two Guilds.

Associations of Guilds of Craftsmen and Merchants were founded in Riga

One of the first Art Nouveau buildings in Riga designed by Alfred Aschenkampff in 1899, 7 Audeju Street

Identity and superstition

A stone camel can be seen above the door on Valnu Street at the Big Camel. This had a dual purpose as warehouses did not have numbers and could easily be identified as the elephant or dove which can be seen on the façade of Sport's Museum No.7. The other reason was superstition, as the Rigans believed such emblems would ward off the evil spirits and protect their merchandise.

during the thirteenth century with the purpose of providing charity to their impoverished members and arranging events like funerals and weddings. A great stimulus to trade was Riga's membership of the Hanseatic League from 1282 to 1630, which gave it close ties to the North German cities like Hamburg, Bremen and Lübeck.

Around the fourteenth century, there was a split in the Guild membership and merchants formed a separate branch under the patron of St Mary leaving the craftsmen who were still part of the St Cross and Trinity Guild. In time, as trade grew between the Hanseatic cities, the **Guild of Merchants** became larger, more influential and its members wealthier than the **Craftsmen's Guild**. The members had the monopoly of trade from the East and the West as they alone could sell goods to locals or foreigners.

Amatu or Craft's Street separates the two guilds. If you walk down the street, the Small Guild is on your left and the Great on your right. At the courtyard next to the house at No.4, a fine example of Wilhelm Bockslaff's Art Nouveau design with men reading books on the roof, there was once a large stone gateway with two entrance arches, one for each guild.

The Small Guild, which with its tower and crenellations looks like a castle, was built in 1866 on the old site and designed by the architect Johann Felsko in what is described as Electic English Gothic style. In the corner of the façade under the little turret is a statue of St John with a lamb. The link to St John dates back to the thirteenth century when members would congregate in Zosta's room, an old house, which once held the former St John's

Reutern family anecdotes

Reutern was so pleased with his house after completion that he gave the architect a silver goblet in appreciation. He was also fined for driving around in a carriage with glass windows, which at the time was considered the height of immorality.

One of the members of the Reutern family, Gerhard Wilhelm, who was a painter and engraver was also a friend of Goethe. He was at the Russian court during the Napoleonic War and served as an adjutant of General Barclay de Tolley. Wounded during a battle he could afterwards only paint with his left hand. Later, he founded the first artists' colony in Germany at Willingshausen in Hessen.

Chapel and from which the guild derived its coat of arms.

In 1888, the interior decoration of the building was completed and its panelled meeting hall on the first floor is particularly outstanding because of the ornamental ceiling and gallery. Stained glass windows were also installed and many depict craftsmen in their traditional costumes, each with their craft's symbol. One window pays tribute to the architect Johann Felsko and the stained-glass artist, Freidstadte from Hanover. In the same picture is a mother and child with an appropriate caption, 'A good wife and your own hearth is worth gold and pearls'. There are also paintings of scenes from other Hanseatic cities on the walls, as well as a selection of framed common sense and wit to rival Ben Franklin's *Poor Richard's Almanac.* Examples include 'Patience, intelligence and time make the impossible possible.'

The Great Guild was reconstructed a decade earlier than its associate, in 1854 and as the members were loath to lose two original parts they were incorporated by the architect, Karlis Beine, in his English Gothic and Monumental Eclecticism building.

The Minster or Münster room which originates from the thirteenth century and was a Franciscan cloister dining-room decorated with Gothic cross vaults is one element that was preserved and it now serves as a foyer of the **Philharmonic Hall** which has taken over the Guild building. The derivation of the room's name is doubtful. Some believe it belonged to merchants from the City of Münster, others claim it is an abbreviation of the word monasterium.

Sinful monks

Two monks' heads with their mouths open are mounted high on the south-west wall and below them is an opening in the wall, covered with a grating. They are symbols of the vain ambition of a couple of Dominicans who wanted to ward off evil on St John's Church and decided to become immured. For a time they lived inside the wall, being fed by passers-by. When they died the Pope did not declare them saints because the church did not benefit from their deaths and pronounced their actions sinful.

It was where the money and documents were kept and was also used as an assembly room.

At the upper end is an old carved figure of the Virgin Mary, under which the Chairman sat on public occasions, that was known locally as the Docke, derived from the Danish Dakke or Doll. According to the John Murray travel guide to Russia in 1893, this could well be the origin of 'dock' in the UK Courts of Law.

The other room that was a first choice with the members and has remained unchanged is the Bride's Chamber which was built in the first half of the fifteenth century. It was used during the joyous occasion of a wedding celebration, which lasted several days and had a nuptial bed to which the newly married couple adjourned after they had danced the first dance. On the eve of the wedding two groups of guests, those of the bride and of the groom, drove in coaches through

Above: Marstalu Street, with Reutern House and its corinthian columned entrance in the foreground and tower of Reformed Church in the background

Left: A view over St Peter's Church towards the canal and parks of the city

A view of Riga Castle from Vansu Bridge showing the presence of the president whose flag is flying from the Holy Ghost Tower

Art Nouveau building

the city twice, each time to the beat of drums and the blowing of trumpets. There is no record of whether the sheets were shown from the windows to the jovial guests the next day!

The square chamber was constructed with richly ornamental star vaults and there is an inscription on the fireplace no doubt for the edification of the couple. 'Do not say things that please people, but speak about things which are of benefit to society'.

We end our walk by following Meistaru Street to the intersection where we began our tour. As a preview of the next tour of the Art Noveau architecture you may wish to stroll down Smilsu Street which is a reminder that the city originated on a sandy peninsula which arose from the Daugava, and its tributary the Ridzene, which has since been filled in. Its outline can still be seen in Kaleju Street.

Since the thirteenth century this street was the most important because it was the continuation of Smilsu Road and sited at the oldest entrance to the city. It is certainly one of the few that has retained its name from earliest times.

Smilsu Road was the main thoroughfare from the countryside and linked villages on the Daugava with the Liv and Latgallian castles on the Gauja river and the craftsmen's settlements around the castle walls. Some stretches were paved with limestone flags, and yards

Walking Path in Kemeri

Guild membership

It was not easy to join a guild and once you bought a house in the city, the Town Council put you on the list of either the Great or the Small Guild. However, it was up to the members to admit you. This could create enmity and an anecdote about the Cats' House at 19 Meistaru Street illustrates the point. A Latvian merchant who wanted to become a member of the Great Guild had his application blackballed. As a consequence of the rejection, he placed two black cats on the towers of his building, each with their tails pointing towards the guild. They soon relented and he changed the animals round to more amenable positions.

along the way with round timber.

During the middle ages Smilsu Street had two public wells and a coal market. Although little of the medieval architecture has remained the street has become a showcase for Art Nouveau styles from 1902 to 1910 and includes the most prominent practitioners such as Konstantis Peksens (at No.2), Wilhelm Bockslaff (at No.6), Heinrich Scheel (at No.8) and Ernests Pole (at No.10).

There are examples too of the master of Eclecticism, Johann Felsko at No's.7 and 12 and the famous Kristofers Haberland has an apartment house at No.5.

Tour Two: Art Nouveau

The Art Nouveau tour covers both the old town and the new city. It is not feasible to see all the buildings and on this walk we will concentrate on the flashy, the elegant and on as many variations of the style as possible.

We begin in **Peitavas Street** with a place of worship, a synagogue, which was the first example of the Perpendicular style and was built in 1904 from the design of the architect and art historian Wilhelm Neumann. It is best seen from the front and although austere in comparison with other buildings the pediment design is successfully echoed in the canopy above the main door and on the side above the two windows; perpendicular derived from the style applied to the Wertheim department store in Berlin.

Moving towards **Kaleju Street**, we turn left into it and follow it round until we reach a ritzy building No.23 which is on the corner with **Jana Street**. The architect, Paul Mandelstamm, who was a leading figure in Eclecticism, Art

Pious admonition

There were also two plaques attached to the gateway which was removed in the middle of the nineteenth century when restoration work was being carried out. One admonished members to lead a good life. 'Dispense with self-interest and its child, envy; discard luxury and abundance; be industrious; live in harmony and moderation' (and if you accomplish this) with God's help you will live a long life'.

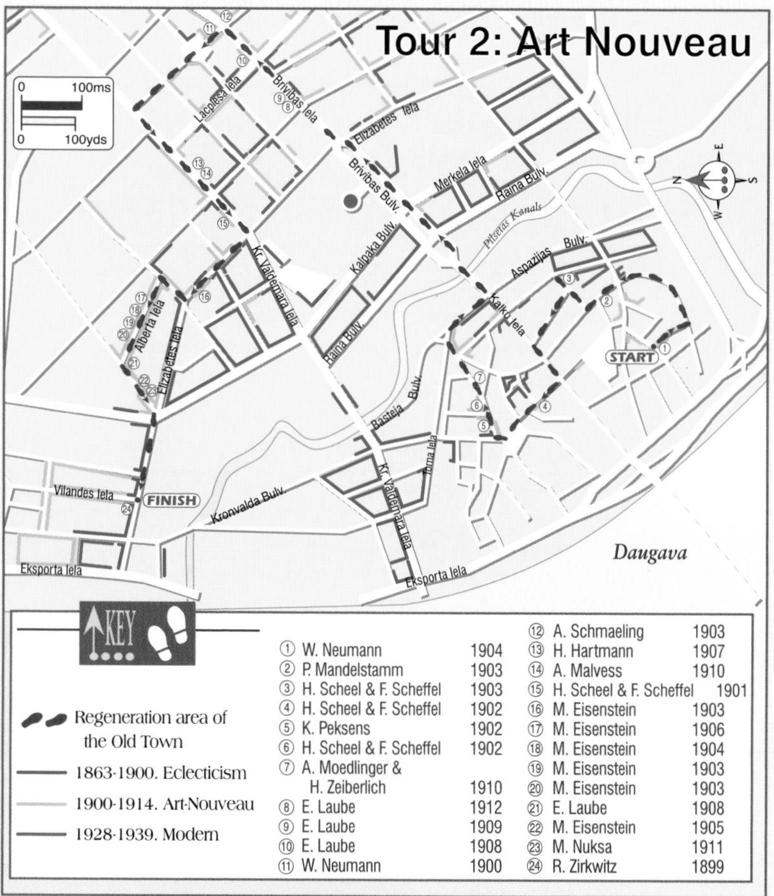

A preference

In Teatra Street (from Kaleju Street) you will find my preferred building designed by architects Scheel and Scheffel which now belongs to the Italian Embassy at No.9. I have to admit that I was not attracted to Art Nouveau at first because I thought it was too elaborate, fussy, excessive but was gradually won over and a turning point was seeing this building from the vantage point of the fifth floor of the Riga Hotel. I had noticed the blue globe glowing at night and was entranced when I saw it in the morning light with sun moving from the globe to the silver rounded tower of the building opposite. Swallows circled in fast flight around this duo and I saw movement in these architectural forms. A strong feature is the cardinal cap roof under the three Atlas figures and the window with arched eyebrow.

Wagner connection

The first Art Nouveau building is No.33, at the corner of Brivibas and Dzirnavu, which has a special significance to music lovers as it was built on the site of a former house where Wagner spent two years (see Music entry). Designed by one of the pioneers of the style, Eizens Laube, the building is rather dark as the façade is clad in black labradorite and is another example of the vertical architecture.

Street we turn right into **Aspazijas Boulevard** and at the **Laima Clock** move towards the Freedom Monument, the most sacred spot for Latvians. The clock is a popular meeting place for lovers. We move around the monument which is in Brivibas Boulevard and towards the Esplanade on our left.

The apartment block at No.37 is also designed by Laube but in the National Romanticism style. Of note is the relief depicting a trio of owls, a triangular balcony and the unusual tiled effect of the peaked roof. The third building by Laube in the street at the corner of Lacplesa Street, No.47, is one of the most outstanding examples of National Romanticism he designed.

One of the first Art Nouveau buildings in the suburbs is found at No.55. A bright orange façade with variations of Dutch gables including one, above the main entrance, with two scrolls. It was built in 1900 and designed by Wilhelm Neumann. The reliefs are the work of Andris Volz.

On the opposite corner at No.68 is a building designed by Alexander Schmaeling three years later, and which attempted to synchronize with No.55 and create an ensemble. There is an interplay of gables and the fine decorative effects on each building complement each other. But the tower with its resemblance to the Dome's tower is no match for the gable with the twin scrolls. The tower with its onion top that can only be seen from several stories up is its most striking feature.

It is at this corner that we turn left down Getrudes Street towards Valdemara. (For those who have been truly bitten by the bug of this architectural style, they may want to walk over three blocks to No.85 and look at Laube's musical masterpiece before joining us again).

When you reach **Valdemara** you turn off into it and head towards No.20. This is quite a conservative building designed by Hermann Hartmann in 1907 and the interesting feature is the use of a band of tiles at the bottom of the low gables. Although the building next door at No.18 is small, its National Romanticism design is effective and should be seen from across the street where it is most striking, particularly the two cowl-like or hooded windows at the top that form part of the roof. The architect was Augusts Malvess and it was built in 1910.

On the way to Elizabetes Street we pass another Scheel and Schaffel building at No.23 the door of which is a splendid example of the use of ironwork in Art Nouveau.

From Elizabetes Street we come to the corner at Antonijas Street and turn right into it before taking the first left into **Alberta Street** which is a highlight of our Art Nouveau tour. Of the five Eisen-stein buildings we will see, four of which are in this street, No.2 is the most beautiful. Built in 1906, the last one in Alberta, it appears to have benefited from his experience. The use of the red tile stripes resembles festive ribbons and provides it with an air of celebration. The five round holes at the top of the façade are like windows open to the sky and on a clear day add blue which he so likes.

Additional effects of the five knights with their visors, up on the uppermost façade and the two sphinxes below, guarding the main entrance, give the building a forceful presence. Two topless belles balance the masculinity. The common part of the interior does not let the exterior down and the décor is soft and graceful to complement it. It is worth entering and the door is usually open. (It is the birthplace of Sir Isaiah Berlin.)

The building at No.4 is a plain version of his style and has great strength in an oval shaped window just below the ovoid pediment with its rampant lions on either side. No tiles are used to embellish it and it should be best seen from across the street. The semi-circular top façade is a particularly successful feature of Art Nouveau such as on Smilsu 3 and Brivibas 72. It was built in 1904, a year before the other two buildings in the street. These were No's.6 and 8, built at the same time, but No.6 appears to fall short of the mark if compared to its sketch which is superior. Perhaps, in the rush to complete both, a wrong decision was made to use red bricks on the façade rather than red tiles which would have been more effective. This can be seen clearly in their use in No.8 where the turquoise tiles brighten the building and make it more prominent than its square box structure would project.

Laube's building at No.11 demonstrates through its gloomy, austere exterior how much of a genius Eisenstein was.

On the way back to Elizabetes Street via **Strelnieku Street** you will see another Eisenstein at No.4a which although elaborate in decorative effects does not surpass any of his masterpieces in Alberta. At No.2, there is another example of how differently this style was expressed in Riga. It was designed by Martins Nuksa in 1911. He was also an ambassador for Latvia who like the architect Mandelstamm met with a tragic end. The top of the façade with crenellations gives an impression of a Spanish fort.

The last stop on the tour is at the corner of Vilandes Street, No.1, a fine example of the early style by Rudolf Zirkwitz. It has been beautifully restored.

First sight of Eisenstein design

In Elizabetes Street we get a foretaste of the grandeur that will come later. At No.10b we see the first brilliant design of Mikhail Eisenstein and its theatrical façade. If there is someone who shines in this style it is him. The use of the blue tiles and the Aztec heads to crown the balustrade of the roof are prominent features. In the original drawing, the tiles on the two top floors were red, a tone which was not used in the end as it would not have been as effective. However, he does use red to great advantage later.

2. In and Around Riga

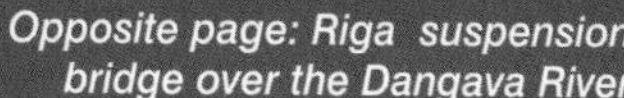

Opposite page: Riga suspension bridge over the Dangava River

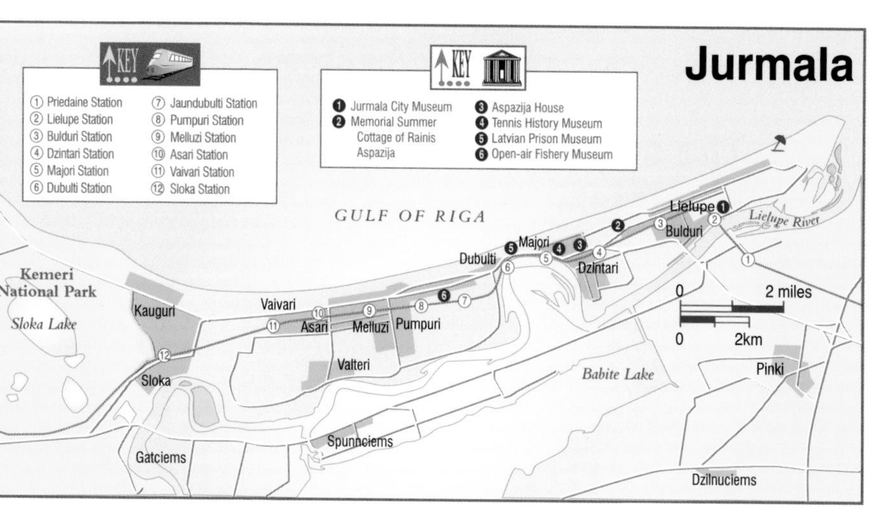

Jurmala Beach

Leaving aside the middle of the city, there are a number of places very close by which are of interest. Perhaps one of the most surprising is the coast.

The seaside Jurmala

Jurmala, which means seaside in Latvian, is one of the secrets about Riga that the Russians knew, that is only now filtering through to the West. The Latvian Riviera is a spectacular wild coast with pine trees bordering on the sandy beaches, where during summer bathers can frolic in the water until evening because of the midnight sun.

Unlike the French and Italian Rivieras, which are built-up areas with promenades and high rises, Jurmala, has the innocence of the African coast. If you are lucky you might find a lone ice-cream cart or a few canvas covered cafés along its 25-mile (45km) long stretch of golden sands.

A geographical feature similar to Miami beach is a river, the Lielupe, running parallel to the shore except for a couple of places when it loops away or inward towards the beach at the main villages Majori and Dubulti. Here the strip of land is only 500yd (457m) wide.

The resort which traces its origins to 1738 when sea bathing was first recorded, consists of a string of fifteen villages. Priedaine is first and nearest to Riga and is located on the banks of the Lielupe river. Here there is an anchorage for yachts. It was built as a residential village for railway workers on the Riga-Orla line. The others Lielupe, Bulduri, Dzintari, Majori, Dubulti, Jaundubulti (new Dub-ulti), Pumpuri, Melluzi, Asari and Vaivari are on the peninsula between the sea and the river. Sloka Kemeri and Jaunkemeri (new Kemeri) are near the sea and the Sloka lake.

Each village has its own character. **Majori** is the liveliest with cafés, art galleries and shops. **Dzintari**, previously called Edinburgh was popular with aristocrats, and its name originated when Maria, the daughter of Tsar Alexander II married the Duke of Edinburgh. At its western end is the summer concert hall, built in 1936 with wall paintings by a local artist Ansis Cirulis, which was extended to include an open-air auditorium.

Lielupe has a yacht club and is a

Russian convalescents

Dubulti is one of the oldest fisherman's villages in Riga bay and during the Napoleonic wars, officers and wounded soldiers would come here to recuperate. Among them was the famous Russian general, Barclay de Tollay who was responsible for the strategy which defeated Napoleon. There was a statue of him on the Esplanade but now only the plinth remains.

sports complex with tennis courts where Davis Cup matches have been held. There are good examples of houses in National Romanticism and Functionalism styles. Due to its remoteness from main villages it was called Australia. **Melluzi**, which is also called Karlsbad after the monocled Baron Firks who owned this village and Majori, is a quiet small place like **Asari** and **Vaivari**, which has an aquatic amusement park.

Dubulti was also the site of the Jewish quarter where Osip Mandelstam would spend holidays with his grandparents. The area between Dubulti and Melluzi was marshy and when it was developed as **Jaundubulti**, wood and gravel was used to strengthen the ground.

Kemeri, which is inland, and **Jaunkemeri**, which is on the bay, are traditional therapeutic places. This is another unique feature of Jurmala for it has been known as a spa and health complex from the time it was opened as a sea resort. Kemeri, which is 4 miles (6km) from the sea, has sulphur springs amongst the surrounding swamps and the locals used the 'holy springs' for medicinal purposes. Foresters first administered the treatment in the healing waters and one of them, Kemers, gave his name to the area.

There is a third compelling reason to visit the Riga seaside – to see examples of the striking wooden architecture both of the nineteenth and twentieth centuries. Of these, 428 buildings have been declared monuments and been included on the project list of UNESCO's world cultural heritage.

Mandelstam's bustling noisy life has found a place in posterity.

Visitors to the seaside first stayed with the local fishermen and farmers who added extensions like terraces and top floors, but during the middle of the nineteenth century, summer cottages were built, particularly when river boat services between Riga and Jurmala gave easy access. The demand for cottages grew after the railway was built in 1877 and gave an impetus to new villages such as Edinburgh, Jaundubulti and Bulduri.

The architectural style during the nineteenth century can be identified by classical elements like columns, pilasters, cornices and pediments. An example of this style can be found in Majori at 43 Jomas Street. The one-floor symmetrical house with monumental columns creates an atmosphere of solemnity but fits in well with the other buildings in the square it faces.

It should be compared with a set of houses on 52-54 Dzintaru Avenue in Dzintari. The main building is a Neo-Gothic asymmetrical structure with turrets, loggias and the unpractical flat roof. The owner, Kristaps Morbergs, added an unusual dimension by covering the wooden framework with copper plates which cause the house to glow at sunset.

A fisherman's cottage built in the early part of the nineteenth century can be seen in Dubulti at 15 Blaumana Street. There is another old example in the same street at No.7 which is crowned with a pediment, classical wooden columns and a semi-circular window.

The most popular style of dacha is Art Nouveau which is usually asymmetri-

Above: Formerly used for spa treatment, eclectic Art Nouveau style, Majori

Opposite: Sailing in the Gulf of Riga

Below: Jurmala beach

Jurmala

There are over thirty springs in Kemeri. Once the mineral waters were examined chemically in St Petersburg, the first state bathing establishment was opened in 1838 through a grant of land by Tsar Nicholas I. Sapropelic mud, which consists of decomposing organic matter, was subsequently discovered in the KanierisLake and is also used in treatments like slimming.

Since then the whole area has become a health resort with over thirty spa hotels offering a variety of rejuvenating cures and thalassotherapies. Many of the hotels have doctors and medical facilities. The mild climate, medicinal mud and sulphurous mineral water combine to make it popular for rest and recreation. The Russian cosmonauts would stay at Vaivari where a special spa was built for them.

It is not unusual for guests to stay for two to three months to undergo treatment or spa cures while on holiday. For example, at the Marienbade in Majori, cardio-vascular and gynaecological diseases are treated as well as metabolic disorders and problems of the nervous system. For as little as £6 or $10 a day the guest can have a consultation with a doctor, mud treatment, medical baths and showers, physiotherapy and acupuncture.

At the Vaivari, which is also the National Rehabilitation Centre, both spa medicine and spa cures are offered. The medical side includes paediatrics, children's orthopaedic surgery, traumatology, neurology, cardiology, plastic surgery and dietology. According to Dr Gundars Rusovs, it is ideal for patients to recuperate after operations, or in the case of stroke victims to help them back to leading as near as possible a normal life. There is a hydro and physiotherapy complex where medical baths, mud procedures and other physical fitness methods are carried out.

I had a water massage, which is unlike any other physio-therapy. You enter a bath twice the size of a normal one, which is filled with warm brownish-hued mineral water. A female attendant runs a hose with water under pressure over your body underwater and the flesh gives way. It is a strange sensation and becomes ticklish when applied to the soles of the feet.

cal, frequently adorned by turrets with iron weathercocks bearing the initial of the owner. A signature of the style is embodied in the **Hotel Majori** which was built in 1925 at 25 Jomas Street and designed by Artur Medlinger. Although purists would argue that the stripes on the first floor typify Classicism and other parts smack of Neo-Baroque, it is nevertheless a good illustration. Another early building is 58 Strelnieku Avenue, (lit 3) Jaundubulti.

There are several other styles like 'Homeland' which derive from Germany (131 Meza Avenue, Lielupe); Neo-Classicism, (2 Juras Steet, Majori), and Romanticism that was stimulated by Latvia's independence (3 Rotas Street, Lielupe). One can see the famous example of the Kemeri hotel (25 Darzina Street, Kemeri) which is one of the most beautiful hotels in Latvia and situated in a landscaped park with garden pavilions, canals, bridges and pathways. Finally there is Neo-Renaissance (3 Valnu Street, Bulduri); Neo-Russian (4 Arijas Street, Asari); Neo-Gothic (Morberg's House, 50152 Dzintaru) and Functionalism (8 Kronvalda Street and 28 Melluza Aveunue, Melluzu).

For readers who enjoy an architectural feast I recommend the book *Architectural Heritage of Jurmala Part 1*, which is written by Richard Petersons and Anita Naudisa.

Most of these buildings have been frozen in time for over fifty years and now are gradually being renovated. However, there has been a recent new addition designed by a top international architect Meinhard von Gerkan who was born in Riga and has a practice in Hamburg. It has all the hallmarks of a Von Gerkan, Marg and Partners building, whether it be a music and conference hall in Lubeck, an airport in Algiers or Hamburg. In essence, there is present a dome or atrium, a textural effect on steel, concrete or glass and an example of modernism in architecture.

The building was commissioned by Victor Krasovitsky and has been described as a deconstructivist Bauhaus house that fits in well with the other dachas as it is a wooden structure. Siberian larch is used outside and interior cupboards, bookshelves and panels are constructed out of cherry wood.

An interesting feature is that it serves as the guest house to an Italianate Villa Marta in which the banker lives. As he likes this particular architectural style, everything in the new house from lamps to furniture is reproduction Bauhaus. The surprise for guests is the central atrium which is an open space for parties. There is a music room with a Steinway grand for concerts, an art gallery with paintings by Malevich, Kandinsky and Miro, a cinema with a huge screen and a library. Outside, between the two houses, is a Japanese garden.

Although the house was primarily planned for visitors, Victor Krasovitsky finds that he and his wife Nina tend to spend more and more time in it because of the interesting interior spaces.

Kemeri National Park

For the tourist who can easily forego beaches and boring buildings but goes weak at the knees at the sight of rare birds, animals and plants then the Kemeri National Park is their place.

Museums in Jurmala

Memorial Summer Cottage of Rainis & Aspazija
5/7 Plieksana Street,
Majori
☎ 776 4295
Open 10am-5pm Monday to Sunday, closed Tuesday.

Jurmala City Museum
27/29 Tirgona Street, Majori
☎ 776 4746
An art museum with representative works of Latvian artists from the past and present. Open 11am-5pm Wednesday to Sunday, closed Monday & Tuesday.

Aspazija House
20 Meierovica Avenue,
Dubulti
☎ 776 9445
Open 11am-4pm Tuesday, Wednesday, Thursday and Saturday, 2-7pm Monday, closed Friday and Sunday.

Latvian Prison Museum
6/8 Piestatnes Street, Dzintari
History of prisons from the Middle Ages to the present.
☎ 775 4536
Open 9am-8pm Monday to Friday, closed Saturday & Sunday.

Open-air Fishery Museum
☎ 775 1121
An unusual excursion to see old fishermans' cottages and fishing equipment, and a trip around a fish factory combined with food tasting.
Open 10am-6pm daily.

It is an amazing nature reserve that includes **Kemeri** and **Jaunke-meri** with wetlands, forests, lakes, villages, lagoons and stretches of coast land. As embodied under law, the area is under state protection and established to maintain the natural, cultural, historical and balneological values and protect the processes of the origin of mineral waters and medicinal mud.

The source of the sulphurous springs was the result of the interaction between dolomite primary rock and a large marsh complex. Another interesting element is the geological structures that connect at this point. Due to the rise of land, the ancient Littorina sea retreated leaving dunes, and coastal lagoons.

Diverse ecosystems maintain the biological diversity of plants and animals. Some twenty-five per cent of the plant species in the Latvian Red data book

Above: Mentzendorff House

Left: The Freedom Monument

Below: Jurmala beach

are found here. This includes 521 types of fungi, 139 lichens, 202 mosses and 894 plants. In the wet forests, spurge, honeysuckle and ramson are found and in the coastal area the great fen sedge, brown bog-rush and bog myrtle. Orchids flourish too in the fens, the early marsh orchid, and the heath spotted orchid among others.

It is also home to over 200 species of birds including the magnificent eagle owl, the white tailed eagle and the whimbrel along the seashore. This should place it as a significant site on the birdwatcher circuit.

Good breeding conditions have encouraged the presence of the black stork which is considered to be a lucky bird in Latvia and special nesting attachments are placed on roofs even at Rundale to attract them *(see page 100)*. The common crane which belies its name as it is not often seen, the lesser spotted eagle and great numbers of the shy corncrakes which are heard rather than seen.

The undisturbed virgin forests have also provided shelter for rare species of woodpeckers – three-toed, middle-spotted and white-backed as well as animals like the wolf, the wild boar, the roe deer and the red deer. Eurasian beaver flourish in the wet areas and the elk prefers the marshes.

Entomologists too will have a field day as there are over 3,000 insect varieties on the site. With wild species of plants and animals disappearing every year worldwide, the Kemeri National Park is a rare place to visit and the scenery is spectacular, particularly the sulphur ponds, boat station and wetlands which from the air look similar to the Okavango deltas.

It is easy to reach from Riga as commuter trains stop at Kemeri station and the Information Centre which is located at the Forest House or **Meza maja** is only a short bus ride away. The address: Meza maja, Kemeri, Jurmala LV-2012, ☎ 776 5386, Fax 776 5040, E-mail kemeri@vdc.lv.

Adolf Zardinsh

One artist found Jurmala's climate (the sunniest place in Latvia) and ambience so much to his liking that he spent thirty years in exile here, from 1937 to 1967, after being turned down as a member of the Art Society in Riga. He was a proficient linguist and spoke English, French and German, besides Latvian and Russian, and filled his diary with comments in any of these languages. Another mainstay during those decades when he dedicated his life totally to art, was his perfect knowledge of the world history of art. Adolf Zardinsh was born in Riga, grew up in Vitesk and retired in solitude to Jurmala. The harder his life became, the more he was inspired by painting and when his works were discovered in an attic in 1997, there were no less than 1,500 paintings he had left to posterity. Be warned how seductive the area is!

The Riga Seaside

As a child, the eminent Russian poet Osip Mandelstam (1891-1938) would be taken by his parents to the Latvian Riviera at the turn of the century. He has a vivid memory of these holidays and has described them in his prose work the Noise of Time.

'The Riga seaside is an entire country in itself. It is famed for its oozy, pure yellow and astonishingly fine sand (even in an hourglass one could hardly find such sand!) and also for the little boardwalks consisting of one or two hole-riddled planks that had been thrown across the 20 versts [Russian unit of measurement] of the villa-dotted Sahara.

'There are no watering places anywhere that can compare with the swing and scope of the dacha life along the Riga coast. The boardwalks, flowerbeds, enclosed front gardens, and decorative glass balls stretch out in a huge endless city, all on a yellow, finely milled, canary sand, such as children play with.

'In the backyards Latvians dry and cure flounder, a one-eyed bony fish, flat as a broad palm. The wailing children, piano scales, the groans of patients from the innumerable dentists' offices, the clatter or crockery in the little resort pensions, the roulades of singers and the shouts to the peddlers – these noises are never silenced in the labyrinth of kitchen gardens, bakeries and barbed wire, and as far as the eye can see along the sand embankment run little toy trains, shod with rails and filled to overflowing with 'hares' who leap about during the trip from prim German Bilderlingshof to congested Jewish Dubbeln, which smelled of swaddling clothes. Wandering musicians strolled about among the sparse pine groves; two convoluted trumpets, a clarinet, and a trombone. Forever being chased away, they blow out their mercilessly false brass note and now here, now there, strike up the equestrian march of the splendid Karolina. [Hares are people who leap on and off moving trams to avoid paying fares.]

'The whole region was controlled by a monocled baron named Firks. He divided his land into two parts; that which had been cleaned of Jews and that which had not. In the clean half, German students sat scraping their beer steins about on small tables. In the Jewish section babies' diapers hung from lines, and piano scales would gasp for breath. In the Germans' Majorenhof there were concerts: Strauss's Death and Transfiguration played by a symphony orchestra in the shell in the park. Elderly German women, their cheeks glowing and their mourning freshly donned found it consoling.

'In Jewish Dubbeln the orchestra strained at Tchaikovsky's Symphonie Pathetique and one could hear the two nests of strings calling back and forth to each other.'

Jurmala beach with Lielupe River on the left

Cultural life of Jurmala

Jurmala, the seaside of Riga, has a lot to offer the visitor and is within half an hour of the city, depending on where you stay. Some may wish to make it their base.

Cultural activities are carried out on a minor scale compared to the city. For businessmen who want to unwind and have fun there is plenty to choose from including tennis, riding, fishing, water sports, yachting, sailing, water-skiing, rowing and hunting. The **Latvian Hunting and Fishing Club** is a good contact and it recommends **Lake Babite**, near Jurmala for fishing. They have a boat that can be hired.

Several museums are spread over six villages and although interesting, the collections are small.

In Majori, the pride of place is the **Memorial Summer Cottage** of the famous Latvian poet, Janis Rainis (1865-1929) and his feminist wife, also a poet, Elza Rozenberga (1865-1943) aka Aspazija. It is a spacious house and also has art Nouveau exhibits, the most spectacular of which is a clock with a nude female sculpture.

Aspazija lived in another house in the next village, Dubulti, for the last ten years of her life. She wrote, "Work is the main nerve of my life. It is my spring revival." A visit there will be interesting as three other noteworthy buildings No's. 20, 36 and 38 are listed on the same avenue, Z Meierovica.

In keeping with the Latvian's oddball choice of museums, Jur-mala has one on tennis, another on prisons, a third on the fishing industry and one devoted to a minor literary figure, Ludins Berzins in Jaundubulti.

The Brothers' Cemetery

I have never visited a military cemetery, as there was never a compelling reason to go. None of my relatives were buried in one and photographs I had seen of Arlington or Normandy depicted rows and rows of neat white crosses, which were off-putting for seeing the real thing. When the Brothers' Cemetery was suggested as a sight, I demurred even though the Latvian Tourist Office tried to persuade me of its worthiness by mentioning that it was a fixture on all Finnish tours. I had heard of the Finns' bibulous nature but not of their interest in morbid things, unless of course they used the visit as an excuse to imbibe more vodka.

However, my curiosity was aroused and as the site was on the way to our destination, the Ethnographic Museum, I agreed to a short stop, particularly as Anda Rezgale, the guide, assured me that there were no graves in the cemetery. If that was the case, I asked myself, why have it?

To be precise, it is an architectural monument, filled with trees and sculptures, and constructed during the heady days of the country's independence. For the first time in several hundred years the nation was free and to celebrate they built the Freedom Monument in the middle of Riga.

The place is more than a commemoration to soldiers who died in both world wars and fighting for independence. It is an expression of the Latvian culture and beliefs.

When Christianity was first brought to the inhabitants of the country by Bishop Albert in the late thirteenth century, he found that they tended to congregate in groves of oak trees to worship. To discourage what he termed pagan practices he cut down all these sacred trees, which also represented men and strength.

The cemetery lies on the outskirts of the city and is easily reached by bus (No.4 or 9) from Brivibas or tram (No.11) from the National Opera stop. It is always open.

You enter the Brothers' rectangular park through an open stone gateway with a carved relief of horsemen on both sides. Their heads hang low as do the regimental flags they carry. Two European lime or linden trees stand on either side of the gateway near the horsemen. According to Latvians, these trees are symbols of females.

The first thing you glimpse as you walk in, is the huge female statue at the other end of the park, which is 500yd (457m) away. As you move towards the series of steps at the halfway mark, you notice a colonnade of fifty oak trees on either side of the wide carpet of cut grass. You mount the staircase to find an altar in which an eternal flame has been placed. Here you pause and look down and understand that the cemetery has been designed on two levels.

Anda points below and says 'Aizsaule' which translated from Latvian means aftersun or the area that describes the place inhabited by the dead. There is no heaven or earth in Latvian beliefs but sun and aftersun.

Mother Latvia is still far away and at her feet lie the two brothers, back to back. The figures are mounted on a wall which is decorated with the coats of arms of all the towns. You move down the steps into a rectangular enclosure, a low wall which is covered with hundreds of square dull plaques with names and dates of soldiers killed during the various wars. There are also some 300 blank plaques for the unknown soldiers who died in the World War II. Again, you see reliefs of horsemen at the point of death, when they have taken a bullet, an arrow or sword thrust to the heart and the horse arcs its neck sensing something strange has happened to the rider. We return at a slow pace and by the time we pass through the gateway, we have walked 1,000yd (1km).

The brief period of independence, a mere two decades, came to an end in 1939 and post-war Latvia became occupied by the Soviet Union. To Sovietise the memorial site, twenty-three Soviet soldiers were buried in the cemetery in 1958. When independence was achieved for a second time, these corpses were removed and the site has become a focus for mass demonstrations every 14 June, the date that commemorates the Stalinist deportations.

As you will see from the Dainas, or songs, Latvian culture customs and beliefs cannot be simply ascribed to paganism. A visit here is a good start to understanding the people, and a moving one. Both the sculptures here and the Freedom Monument are the work of Karlis Zale.

The Freedom Monument

The other national shrine is Milda, the nickname for the Freedom Monument,

Above: Jomas Festival

Below: Livu Aquapark, fun for all the family

Above: Sunset

left: Pines

Below: Pegasa Pils hotel

Defending the monument

The Soviet authorities attempted to take down the monument on several occasions but the Rigans protected it vigorously against such action. They then resorted to other tactics and allowed traffic to move around the monument and made it illegal for the locals to approach it. Some did and placed flowers at the base, an act that resulted in deportation to Siberia or loss of jobs.

which was finished in 1935, a year before the Brothers' cemetery. Sited on the edge of the Old City at the Junction of Brivibas and Raina Boulevard this is another expression of exuberance during the heady days of Independence, it is the Latvians' equivalent of the Statue of Liberty.

There is no torch in her right hand or tablet in her left, nor a poem extolling the tired, the poor and the huddled masses; but Milda instead holds three golden stars aloft, each representing a province of the country with an inscription reading 'for Fatherland and Freedom'. The tall, long-legged figure accurately depicts the types of females you find in the city.

It is a focal point on 18th Nov-ember, National Independence Day, where the Prime Minister and President review the armed forces. Friezes around the square base show ordinary men and women singing and working while soldiers fight for freedom. Two guards of honour stand to attention at the front of the base. Milda, which occupies the former site of a statue of Peter the Great who had bought a house in the city, is hollow inside and it is possible to walk up to the top where a window offers a splendid view. However, the entrance is closed.

Salaspils Concentration Camp Memorial

When I was told that I was going to stay as a guest with a famous Latvian writer, who lived in Sal-aspils, I was somewhat dismayed. This was the site of a former Nazi concentration camp. I imagined that the town, some 9 miles (15km) south-east of Riga, was close to the camp and that the buildings would resemble those of Auschwitz and Belsen. I was mistaken on both counts. The town was nowhere near the camps, which had been carefully hidden by the Nazis in a forest, and all the buildings had been razed to the ground. The camp can be reached by train, alighting at Darzinia station and following a footpath for about fifteen minutes.

The memorial erected on the site of the camp is both dramatic, and successful as outdoor sculpture. Other holocaust monuments in the US and Europe are different and not as effective because they are too abstract and minimal-ist in their conception. Here both the figurative and abstract elements work harmoniously and the horror of the event is etched on your mind through giant statues in a simple way. The titles are meaningful; the broken, the humiliated, solidarity and Mother Latvia.

A naked woman, so often seen in snapshots, on private film of the executions taken by soldiers, is shown kneeling. You see the outline of her back and buttocks and the Linden tree planted nearby partly covers her body for modesty. In the foreground, to the right is a man lying on the ground with his torso slightly raised. Such a stance reveals an unbroken spirit even as he lies dying. Behind him in the background, stand three men; one with his fists raised while another supports a weaker colleague. Then right at the back of this group, situated in 99 acres (40 hectares), stands a defiant Mother Latvia. Not in a consoling role as she is in the Brothers' Cemetery, but confronting the threat to her people, who, as children, shelter behind her.

An abstract counterpoint to these figures is an oblong black marble block which is positioned some way in front of the kneeling woman. As I strolled in this Gulliver landscape on a warm sunny day in May enthralled by it all, I was disturbed by a knocking sound. It was a pesky sound of a hammer on stone. I looked for the source, but only saw a woman placing flowers on a gravestone in an adjacent cemetery, and then as I moved towards the marble block, I then understood that the sound emanated from a hole in the stone. The penny dropped, this was a buried metronome.

I soon forgot about the irritant when I saw a little daisy-chain garland, and four bunches of flowers including red carnations, lying against the dark stone. A beautiful and poignant reminder of a loving link with the past.

The entrance to this field of giants is under a long concrete block half sunken into the earth at one end and resting up against a huge black base at the other. There are many notches in the base, and the only explanation I have is that each notch represents a day of the camps existence. Black letters are written across the angled concrete block and are from a Latvian poet, Eizens Veveris, who was imprisoned there. 'Behind this entrance the earth moans'.

On the way back, I found steps inside the block which led to a view at the top, when you exited at the bottom to a small display of about ten illustrations of different parts of the camp. There were thirty-nine barracks on the site between 1941-1944 where Jews and other prisoners of war were murdered. Salaspils was one of several labour camps and stones mark the perimeter.

3. City Art Galleries & Museums

Opposite: The Latvian Photographic Museum

There is a wide range of museums and art galleries in Riga. Details of locations and opening times for all those mentioned here can be found in the panel at the end of this chapter.

Art in Latvia

Art ranks high in Latvian culture which has produced notable portraitists, abstract painters, like Mark Rothko, and a top collector – Jospeh Hirshhorn, who endowed a museum and sculpture garden in Washington.

The tradition of Latvian painting dates back to the court of the Duke of Courland in the eighteenth century. Portraits of Ernest Johann painted by Caravaque and of his son Peter and his daughter-in-law Dorothea with children are by the artist Friedrich Barisian. Other prominent painters followed down the centuries including Eggink, Döring, Grass, Bertins, Roze, Feders and Alksnis until you reach Janis Rozentals (1866-1916) who is considered to be the founder of Latvian painting. Son of a blacksmith, Rozentals was a member of Rukis which included other talented people such as Vilhelm Purvitis who became internationally known because of his impressionistic canvases and Arturs Baumanis. The **State Museum of Art** has examples of their works and it is impressive to get this long historical perspective.

Another group of artists called the French circle rebelled against the Soviet regime through their Francophilia in the 1950s. One member Kurts Fridrihsons, was sent to Siberia while another in the 1960s, Imants Lancmanis was ordered to restore Rundale. The palace had deteriorated badly and had been used partly as a grain store and a boarding school. The splendid renovation was the making of Lancmanis as he achieved the impossible.

Painting has always been a strong suit of the country compared to the surrounding countries, Lithuania where sculpture has prevailed, and Estonia which has been foremost in high-tech cool intellectual forms of expressions like architecture and video installations. As a result, it has produced one of the world's top abstract artists Mark Rothko who was born in Daugapils.

Latvia's top ten artists

The doyenne of Latvian art is Laima Slava, an art historian who established the publisher, Neputns, with its list of art books and is also the publisher of the three influential magazines on fine art, design and photography. Everything that goes on in these fields, and for a small country, there is a good deal, can be found in Studija, Fotos and Design Studija. Although, she never publishes a list of top artists and photographers, she made one available for our guide.

1. Katrina Neiburga. An artist that uses personal experiences and images from pop culture to reveal contemporary human being. A graduate of the department of visual communication at the Latvian Academy of Art, she constantly returns to self-examination and Spamatex is an exemplar of this process. A departure is the interesting work called Teashroom (2000/2001 with P_ teris _imels and Kaspars Vanags) which is a multi-media project that used video, photos and publications. It went even further as a shop, a website, a newspaper and an advertising campaign was created to fulfill the concept. Visitors to the Teashroom shop could taste the drink made from this fungus and purchase a piece of the Teashroom in order to continue to grow it at home. They could obtain further information on growing this fungus, its properties and positive effects on the organism as well as read "Teashroom", the newspaper published by the "Latvian Teashroom Growers' Association press organ" and meet fellow enthusiasts and exchange hints and tips on growing the fungus. There was also an advertising campaign that promoted the Teashroom like any other consumer product and encouraged its cultivation at home. "Teashroom" is a complex project envisaged as a critique of consumer society using its manipulative mechanisms – shop, advertising campaign, newspaper, Internet. "Teashroom" was intended to be a "Trojan horse at the gates of the con-

A photograph of Andris Grants

sumers' walls", but also as propaganda for a healthy and natural lifestyle with the slogan "Teashroom against Coca-Colaisation!" It was also an attempt to counter the "negative attitude towards environment protection, the progressively ever-increasing volumes of production, the role of chemicals in the daily diet and the achievements in bioinformatics technologies."

2. Gints Gibrans. A conceptual artist who encapsulates multi-angles of perception.

3. Girts Muiznieks. The essence of his work is painting itself which based on colour and the ability to radiate an emotionally charge of energy.

4. Inta Ruka. A photographer who does portraits of ordinary people I'm the city and coutryside.

5.Ilmars Blumbergs. A stage designer with significant contributions to painting.

6.Andris Grants. A photographer who captures moments and immortalises them.

7.Alnis Stakle. A photograper who sets compositions perfectly that metaphors the use of this medium means.

8.Ieva Iltnere. A painter whose work is a real delight for those who are interested in aesthetics.

9.Janis Avotins. The main theme of his painting is the fundamental solitude of human existence

10. Giebs Panteiejevs. A sculptor who shows extreme care towards material and textures.

Ieva Iltnere

Ieva Iltnere lives in the fashionable quarter of the Right Bank, Kalku Street, in a large photographic studio. The living room, which has a view of the promenades below, is half the size of the studio at the back, where we stand and look at her latest painting on the easel, a double portrait of a woman with tears. The light streams in on this autumn evening not from south-facing windows but from a glass roof. Mounted paintings are stacked against one wall, with their canvas backs towards us.

She was inspired by Man Ray's famous photograph of eight tears on a woman's face.A photograph is a significant element in her work, particularly when it captures an emotional moment which is transposed into a painting. Two versions of the tearful woman, a blue and white sketch and another in violet form the latest work. 'Without emotions no one will find your work interesting' she said in reference to this tearful theme, which reminded me of Kiki Smith's Mother, in which a cast of glass feet is mounted above some thirty large glass tears. 'The human factor always works.Why hasn't painting died out? Because it is unique, created by human hand and seen with human eyes'.

One of the articulate artists in Latvia, she has pondered the *fin de siècle* and with frankness expressed her apprehension.

'I got the feeling that as we approach the millennium' she explained, 'everything is happening at an accelerated pace. I can envision it as water flowing out of a bath.When it is full you don't even notice it, but towards the end the vortex spins faster and faster. We are now at the stage when the bath is almost empty. Purely visually now I'm frightened by the number 2000.'

'There is something I don't like about it – until I get used to it. Something new and unknown awaits. But in reality probably nothing special will change. So much has changed already, if we look back since 1991 (the date of Latvia's independence from the Soviet Union). It's a relative thing, but life has become more merciless'.

Laima Kaugure

Applied art has always been a strong suit of the Latvian character and weaving has predominated over the centuries because of its practicability and as a medium where women could express their creativity.It became the most popular folk art and each region had its specific traditional design for textiles. Laima Kaugure comes from this background - both she and her mother were weavers, and she studied textiles at the Academy of Art. At the beginning of her career, she made wool and silk tapestries and paintings on silk but in 1995 she was inspired by by another natural

Laima Kaugure

fibre, flax. Although, she revived old weaving techniques – in her studio women still work on those wonderful wooden-frame looms, she has achieved a breakaway from the traditional use of linen with coarse, thick texture and grey and beige colours with her modern colourful design and range of airy, transparent fabrics. As a result, she has transformed the end use and bed

Gints Gabrans work

The Latvian Sports Museum in housed in a 17th century warehouse

and table linen or curtains and blinds will never be the same again. Single-handedly, she has also turned linen garments and accessories like shawls into sought-after fashion items through her elegant and chic touch and creation of fabric combinations with wool, silk and metal.There is no surprise that Giorgio Armani and Calvin Klein are clients and have custom-made collections.

"I like linen because of its timeless and magical connection between people and nature and the past and the present," she said.

Linen is about lifestyle. It has special characteristics that cools in summer, warms in winter and at night, there is the sensual experience of linen sheets. Above all, the natural fabric allows your body to breathe. Laima Kaugure in her range Studija Naturals shows it at its best.

Art Collectors

The top entrepreneur, Valerijs Kargins has all the paintings of K Rosens and exclusively collects works by artists up to World War II, while Victor Krasovitsky is awash with L L Lieberts, a Maurice Utrillo figure who painted scenes mostly from postcards. Top bankers such as Dr Kari Nars, Director of the European Bank of Reconstruction and Development are assembling collections of Latvian abstract artists.

Modern painters are also in demand and can be found in galleries like Agija Suna, Bastejs. Daugava Noah (a floating non-profit art gallery near the Radisson SAS hotel), M6 Art Gallery and Rigas. The Volmar art and antiques shop has a unique collection of over 1,000 canvasses of a forgotten artist, Adolf Zardinsh whose work was found some thirty years after his death.

'It is a miracle' said Janis Borgs 'similar to the discovery of a new island in the Baltic. His paintings have been described as Chagall-like and they look good in electric light as they were usually painted in a windowless room.

Museums in Riga

Riga Motor Museum

When I heard that the only motor museum in the former Soviet Union was in Riga, the Latvian capital, I was not surprised. Russia's first car factory, the Russo-Baltic, was built there in 1909. I expected to find the Riga Motor Museum car collection housed in a Stalinist mausoleum. Instead, the building resembled a modern car showroom with a huge radiator grille as its façade.

Victors Kulbergs, founder of the Antique Automobile Club, initiated the idea in 1986. The goal was to collect and restore veteran, vintage and classic cars, motorcycles and bicycles. Today the museum's many exhibits are displayed on two floors above restoration workshops

Edvins Liepins, the current director, added another category to the collection – racing cars. But the museum's other outstanding feature consists of the vehicles of former Soviet leaders bought for a pittance from the Kremlin garage. Stalin, Khrushchev, and Brezhnev are represented by their 'wheels', and lifelike wax models.

Stalin sits at the back of his protected 1949 ZIS 115, his boots on his foot-rest, protected by three inch thick windows and steel plates all round. When each door was closed he drew a chain across to lock it like the security in hotel rooms. The car sports a chrome grille, three headlights, one in the middle of the radiator, a radio aerial above the windscreen and a Soviet insignia on the bonnet – a red flash with a silver star. Although very heavy, its 182 horsepower tuned engine made it the fastest car at the time. 'When the car was exhibited in Germany,' said Liepins, 'I had to share my room with Stalin's wax head. It was an eerie experience as he looked so real I could even see the freckles on his face.'

Brezhnev, who liked collecting and driving fast cars, sits in his 1965 Rolls-Royce Silver Shadow, a gift from President Richard Nixon. The car has been retained with the damage it suffered in a collision with a mammoth truck. The former Soviet leader – and his elegant machine – emerged almost unscathed from the accident. There were a couple of cracks in the passenger window and a slightly bent steering wheel. The front end took the greatest impact and the engine appears under the crushed bonnet.

A waxwork Krushchev stands next to a 1965 ZIL with its four headlights, panorama windscreen and V8 engines. To complete this political collection is the trophy car, the 1937 Rolls-Royce with an aluminium body, captured from the Germans during World War II and presented by Stalin to Molotov.

'The only car that is missing from this amazing collection is Lenin's Rolls-Royce,' says Tom Krooswijk, vice-president of Intercontinental Hotels. 'In this early model the two Rs of the insignia are red and not black. It's in his museum in Moscow.'

Another trophy car that the Soviet army brought back during the war was King Carol II of Romania's 1937 Special Packard Super with French Franay coachwork and a Detroit chassis.

Quality restoration is carried out on site and the low working costs have attracted business from collectors as well as car manufacturers' museums, including Audi's. The Russian cars in the collection include the tall ZIL (which incidentally is translated from Russian as 'named after Ligachov', one of the directors of the car company). Besides the 1980 Gaz, there are cars from the 1950s, the Moskvic, the Volga Gaz, the Pobeda (Victory) and the Gaz 12 ZIM, which is derived from a Cadillac design. In terms of the sophistication of their engines and the speed they could achieve, these machines were about twenty years behind equivalent cars built in the West.

German cars are another strength of the collection and include the only veteran car, a 1914 Hansa. This is a two-seater with exposed suspension and two carbide headlamps. The gas generating block for the lights is on the left running board, while on the right you find the reserve petrol tank and 'hunting horn' hooter. The steering wires are also exposed and resemble a child's go-kart design, connected only to the right-hand wheel.

Mercedes Benz, BMW, Horch and Opel cars are represented in the collection. The 1937 290 Mercedes has a comfortable interior and a good view of the road. It was fitted with a 12-volt electro system. The 68 horsepower engine had a top speed of 65mph (103kph).

The BMW 328, built a couple of years later, was even more efficient in terms of its powerful performance. Its 80 brake horsepower engine produced speeds up to 90mph (145kph). It is one of only 462 to be built.

For devotees of the classic Karmann Ghia marque, which made such an impact with its hardtop coupé design in the 1960s, the 1938 Adler two-litre EV will be of great interest. The upper part of this sleek and uncommon car is produced by the company, while the chassis and engine are from the Adler works.

There are four good examples of Horchs, three from 1939 and one from 1936, an 853. Of these, two are coupés and the saloon, an 830, is for sale at $100,000. This could be a bargain as

Stalin's armoured car in the Riga Motor Museum

the museum values its 1936 model at $200,000 or more. Both the Horchs and an open-top 1939 Opel Admiral with the body made in the famous Glaser Coachworks, are from the private collection of one of the top classic car owners, Egils Martinsone.

One of the most attractive cars in the collection is the 1938 Steyr 220 from Austria, which has an almost perfect aerodynamic body. With its 55 horsepower, six-cylinder engine, it could successfully compete against the larger BMW 327 with an 80 horsepower engine.

Among American cars in the collection is a 1929 De Soto, a 1934 Lincoln owned by the Russian writer Maxim Gorky and a beautifully restored red 1930 Ford A roadster. There are oddities such as a 1949 Tatra with a fin design from Czechoslovakia and the 1965 NSU Spider with Wankel engine.

Open-air Ethnographic Museum

Open-air museums are not a well-liked venue but the Ethnographic Museum is more like a natural theme park. At weekends the visitor can see farmers, weavers, carpenters, blacksmiths, bee-keepers and potters at work and at the same time get an idea of the traditional ways of life between the sixteenth and nineteenth centuries. There are reconstructions of old and ancient buildings from the four regions of the country and a taste is also given of the various regional fashions as participants dress in folk costumes.

The museum was founded in 1924 and the site chosen is ideal as it is placed in a pine forest alongside Lake Jugla which is a typical habitat in the country. The first building was an eighteenth

Above: Museum of Decorative & Applied Art and St George's Church

Below: Jurmala Open Air Museum

century threshing barn and now there are over 120 buildings, of which the oldest is a sixteenth century wooden church that is hand painted inside in natural tones. The door is of particular interest, as it resembles a sergeant's V-strips shown in red rather than gold.

As visitors wander around the 247-acre (100-hectare) site, they will find organic forms. One thatched family home even had a special wheel on the roof for storks to nest. It was sunk low into the ground and had the largest thatched roof I have ever seen. Again wooden buildings predominate including windmills, there are beehives made out of hollowed-out trunks mounted on stones and farming implements. There is also an example of old wooden sauna which has been used since time immemorial by the Latvians as a maternity ward – it is warm and hygienic. In summer you can swim in the lake and in winter skate on the surface. If you are short of time to make an excursion outside Riga, this will do well as a substitute. It is a popular venue for Ligo.

The Jewish Museum

The link between Latvia and the Jews began as early as the fifteenth century when Jews were permitted to come to Riga on business for limited periods and were permitted to stay in special inns called 'Judenherberge'.

The Jewish Museum or Holocaust Centre, was founded by a group headed by the historian, Marger Vestermanis, who was a former prisoner in the Riga ghetto and the Kaiserwald concentration camp. Housed in two rooms on the third floor, it is principally a photographic exhibition and 'a memorial of the world that perished forever in torments and suffering' according to the curator, Lia Gherman. But there are also relics from different periods from the last world war. There is a huge framed Nazi map which shows the Baltic countries with the words 'Judenfrei' (Free of Jews) printed across them. To substantiate this statement a symbol of coffins is used with numbers of the Jews killed alongside in each country. A video of a film, made by a Nazi soldier, of an ethnic cleansing action can be seen on request.

There are also fine examples of how ordinary Latvians helped to save Jews at the expense of their own lives. Venerated are Zanis Lipke, Elvira Rone, Arturs Motmillers, Anna-Alma Polis and Andrejs Graubins. Some 150 Jews were saved and of the five rescuers, two – Anna-Alma Polis and Andrejs Graubins, perished.

A pamphlet, *Fragments of the Jewish History of Riga* includes a walking tour, with scholarly notes, of eighty-five sites and covers over three and a half centuries.

There is a thread running through the museum that dem-onstrates the significant role Jews had in Latvian society and the contribution they made in the arts, sports, political and intellectual life. Sir Isaiah Berlin who was born there is mentioned but not Mark Rothko which is an oversight.

State Museum of Art

The building was designed by Vilhelms Neimans, who was also the State Museum of Art's first director, and was built in the early 1900s to house collections from the Riga Art Museum and the Art Advancement Society. The influence of the Art Nouveau can be seen in the interior, particularly the banisters. It is the main re-pository of Latvian art from the eighteenth century to 1945 and has over 14,000 works including paintings, sketches and drawings.

The impetus for national art came from the second director, Vilhelmus Purvitis, the well-known landscape artist.The first floor contains Baltic and Russian paintings, including those of Nicolai Rerih, from the eighteenth to mid-nineteenth centuries.The second floor covers a chronological perspective of Latvian art from the mid-nineteenth century to the end of World War II.The ground floor has a mixture of Latvian and Russian portraits and landscapes. Of note is the portrait of singer Malvine Vignere-Grimberga by Janis Rozentals (1916).

J Rozentals and R Blaumanis Memorial Museum

Janis Rozentals (1866-1916), a graduate of St Petersburg Academy of Arts, and Latvia's most famous painter lived in what is now the **J Rozentals and R Blaumanis Memorial Museum** for eleven years from 1904-1915 before he escaped with his wife to Helsinki. He and his wife, a Finnish singer, had an artistic salon at the address. Rudolfs Blaumanis, a playwright, rented a room there for two years from 1906-8. Although Rozentals painted some 300 works, a small oeuvre is on show as well as photographs.

The Museum of Decorative and Applied Art

A visit is worthwhile, as there are two features of interest: the Museum of Decorative and Applied Art with exhibits of splendid porcelain, tapestries and woodcuts and the building itself which is the oldest stone building in the city. St George's Church, built early in 1200 and cited in the Livonian Indrikis Chronicle of 1209, was the chapel of The Knights of the Sword's first Riga Castle called Witgenstein because of the hue of the white stone. It ceased to be a place of worship during the Reformation when Catholic buildings were destroyed and was rebuilt in 1689 when it was used as a warehouse.

There are three exhibition spaces and the curator, Ilze Martinsone, has used them well.The first floor (where church services were once held) is used for new shows. On the second and third floors are permanent collections of applied art from the nineteenth to the twentieth century. Work of the most prominent artists of the 1920s and 1930s, such as the erotic art of Sigismunds Vidbergs, and interior décor of Ansis Cirulis are on show on the second floor. Examples from the porcelain painting studio called Baltars can also be seen. Of note is an Art Deco wedding plate designed by Romans Suta in 1928, and a superb sculpture titled *The Swimmer* by Stefans Bercs.

Museum of Foreign Art

The Museum of Foreign Art is a great surprise for it is housed in Riga Castle in halls with thirteenth century vaulted ceilings. It originated when the City of Riga was given Nikolaus Himsel's collection of paintings in 1773. He was a physician and art collector. There is an eclectic collection, from Ancient Egypt and Greece to paintings of Belgian artists of the 1930s. Some galleries are provocative as sculptures and curios from the ancient world are mixed with modern examples. Most Euro-pean artists from England, the Netherlands and Germany during the sixteenth to twentieth cen-turies are represented, including drawings by Rembrandt and Goya. The key seems to be variety and minor rather than major works. Frieda Kahlo, the Mexican painter, is also represented as well as ceramics, glass, bronze, china and textiles. It also has a unique Meissen porcelain collection.

Opposite top: A poster advertising the Song Festival of 1938

Arsenals Art Museum

The building housing the Arsenals Art Museum was designed by two St Petersburg architects, Lukini and Nel-linger, in 1832 and was constructed to serve as a customs storehouse. It is a good example of classical style and offers a large selection of Latvian and European paintings, sculpture and

Below: Interior St George's Church, part of exhibition floor of Museum of Decorative & Applied Art

decorative art. Of note is Fanis Pauluk's (1906-1984) portrait of Felicita with Sunshade.

Museum of History of Riga and Navigation

The Museum of History of Riga and Navigation has fine examples of Art Nouveau furniture, china, glass and applied arts. Of particular interest are birch chairs veneered with mahogany, a Kusnetsow ceramic dessert dish, glass vases from the local Ilguciems factory and picture frames.

Latvian Photography Museum

The permanent exhibition of the Latvian Photography Museum illustrates the development of photography in Latvia from 1839 to 1941. There are early examples of historic processes like daguerreotypes, and cameras including the smallest camera in the world (1930s), the VEF-Minox which would have been standard equipment for spies. Photography exhibitions are mounted monthly.

Museum of Latvian Culture

The museum is of dual interest as the house in which it is dis-played was owned by a brewer, A Bringners, and has been restored and is worth seeing. A collection of items reflecting Latvian culture is exhibited. It was also the residence of President Karlis Ulmanis.

History Museum of Latvia

This is a good museum run by Professor Arnis Radins. He has a wealth of material, some 600,000 objects, from the Stone Age to the present. It is interesting that the Latvians originated from four tribes, the Livonians, Semigallians, the Latgellians and the Selonians, and inhabited the Baltic together with the Baltic-Finnish people, the Estonians and Livs. Their territory spread east as far as Moscow. The Slavs only appeared on the scene as late as 700AD.

Occupation Museum of Latvia

Last but not least is the museum is dedicated to the Nazi and Soviet occupation of Latvia.

Places to Visit

Art Galleries

Agija Suna

9/11 Kaleju Street
☎ 708 7543
Open 11am - 6pm, closed Sun.

Artist Union of Latvia

11 Novembra Kr
☎ 722 8997
Open 11am - 5pm, closed Sun & Mon.

Bastejs

12 Basteja Boulevard
☎ 722 5050
Open 12 - 6pm Mon to Fri, 12 - 4pm Sat, closed Sun.

Daugava

7 Jana Yard
☎ 721 2896
Open 10am-6pm, closed Sunday.

Noah

A B Dambis opposite Radisson SAS Hotel
☎ 7703240
Ring to check exhibitions and opening times.

Riga's L Galerija

20 Aspazijas Boulevard
☎ 722 5887
Open 12 - 7pm, closed Sun.

Volmar (art and antiques)

6 Skunu Street
☎ 721 4278
Permanent exhibition of Adolf Zardinsh. Open 10am - 7pm.

Museums

Riga Motor Museum

6 Eizensteina Street
☎ 253 7730
Open 10am - 6pm Tue to Sun, closed Mon.

Open-air Ethnographic Museum

440 Brivibas Street
☎ 799 3306
Open 10am - 5pm daily.

The Jewish Museum

6 Skolas Street
☎/Fax 728 3484
Open 12 - 5pm Mon to Fri, closed weekends.

State Museum of Art

10a K Valdemara Street
☎ 732 5021
Open 11am - 5pm, closed Tue.

J Rozentals and R Blaumanis Memorial Museum

12 Alberta Street (the entrance is in Strelnieku Street)
☎ 733 1641
Open 11am-5pm Mon, Tue and Sun, 12 - 7pm Fri and Sat, closed Tue and Wed.

The Museum of Decorative and Applied Art

10–20 Skarnu Street

☎ 722 2235/7833
Open 10am - 5pm every day except Mon.

Museum of Foreign Art

3 Pils Square
☎ 722 6467
Open 11am - 5pm, closed Mon.

Arsenals Art Museum

1 Torna Street
☎ 721 3695
Open 11am - 5pm, closed Mon.

Museum of History of Riga and Navigation

4 Palata Street
☎ 721 2051
Open 11am - 5pm Wed to Sun, closed Mon and Tue.

Latvian Photography Museum

8 Marstalu Street (entrance from Alksnaja Street)
☎ 722 7231
Open 1-7pm Wed & Thur, 11am - 5pm Fri, 11am - 3pm Sat, closed Sun, Mon and Tue.

Museum of Latvian Culture

30 Sarkandaugavas Street
☎ 739 2229
Open 11am - 5pm, closed Tue.

History Museum of Latvia

3 Pils Square, Riga Castle
☎ 722 3004
Open 11am - 5pm, closed Mon and Tues.

The Occupation Museum of Latvia

1 Strelnieku Square
☎ 721 2715
Open 11am - 5pm daily.

Riga Porcelain Museum

9/11 Kaleju iela
☎ 7503769
11–6pm.

Stradins Museum of Medicine

1 Antonijas iela
☎ 7334223
11–5pm
Closed Sun & Mon.

4. Excursions from Riga

Opposite: The Red Study next to the Duke's bedroom

Rundale Palace

The Rundale Palace rivals Louis XIV's Versailles and you can find interesting echoes of the Sun King's motifs throughout.

Outside in the cobble-stoned courtyard, horses and carriages drove over a design of the sun with rays while the formal gardens were laid out with wide paths radiating towards the park. Inside, the Duke's bedroom is placed in the middle of the main buildings giving dominant views over the gardens and courtyard, enabling him to spy on the comings and goings. The bedroom is decorated with a sun symbol on the ceiling. Another solar feature is the interspersion of round windows in the attic of the quadrangular building.

History of Rundale

The Baroque and Rococo masterpiece belies a story of love, intrigue and power. It begins with Anna Ivanova, the daughter of Peter the Great's imbecilic brother, who was married off by her uncle at the age of seventeen to the Duke of Courland, Frederick William.

On the way back from St Peters-burg to Jelgava (then known as Mitau), the

Visit details

Rundale Palace, Pilsrundale, LV-3921, Latvia

Highlights

- Excellent example of Rastrelli's work which is on a par with the Winter Palace and Versailles, albeit on a smaller scale
- Superb renovated halls and rooms
- Original wooden staircase
- Only just over an hour's drive from Riga

If you need a royal recommendation, Queen Margrethe of Denmark has said it is 'One of the most beautiful palaces in Europe'

Open daily from 10am to 6pm from May to October, and from 10am to 5pm from November to April 396 2197, Fax 396 2274. The halls are available for functions such as weddings and birthdays. You can book meals in the

Duke died and Tsar Peter ordered his reluctant niece to take over the government with the Russian president, Count Peter Bestuzhev, as her advisor. This was the original motive as it gave the Tsar an opportunity to gain a foothold in the Polish Kingdom. For a brief period, she was the Count's mistress before she met the love of her life, Ernst Johann Biron (or Bürhren) who also became a lifelong friend and counsellor.

Ernst Biron

He was an ambitious adventurer who was expelled from Konigsberg University for riotous conduct before setting out to seek his fortune in Russia. But having failed he returned to Jelgava where he met Anna through his sister, who was also the mistress of Bestuzhev. He was three years older, and the grandson of a groom on the estate. He later married Benigna von Trotta-Treiten, one of her ladies-in-waiting and they had three children.

After the death of Peter the Great in 1730, Anna Ivanova was invited to return to Russia as Empress. On her acceptance of the Russian crown, she was forced by the supreme privy council to subscribe to nine articles that reduced her powers as a monarch. She bided her time and on 8 March, in a *coup d'état,* overthrew the council and was hailed an autocrat. Biron joined her in Moscow and she showered him with riches and veneration at her coronation in May. He was appointed Grand Chamberlain, given the title of count and an estate with an income of 50,000 crowns a year.

He became the all-powerful adored-one, and in keeping with the position, adopted the French ducal house of Biron and ruled the country in her name. Her government, through his outrageous insolence particularly towards the Russian nobility, was universally unpopular. Contemporary diplomatic sources depict him as mean, treacherous, vindictive and rapacious, and half the bribes intended for the court ended up in his coffers.

When the Winter Palace was completed as a main residence for the Empress he asked her if the renowned architect Bartholomew Rastrelli could build him a summer palace in south Latvia. She agreed and as he had acquired the bankrupt Rundale Estate, Rastrelli was dispatched to the site. It was a tremendous task but Biron was fortunate in the choice of the architect. He had extraordinary organisational skills and was one of the most energetic and talented men of his time.

The foundation stone was laid in the same year 1736, when Anna Ivanova's Winter Palace was completed and this enabled Rastrelli to focus entirely on Rundale. Designs are still to be seen

Construction statistics

In 1735 over 1,000 craftsmen, as well as Russian soldiers, were involved in the construction. The mammoth scale of the operations was reflected in the calculation that to transport some three million bricks, 12,000 logs, 16,000 lime barrels and other materials, some 433 wagon loads were needed daily.

today as they are lodged in the drawing repository of the Albertina in Vienna. Rastrelli was as busy as ever, he even designed the coat of arms, but an event occurred which luckily would bestow two Rastrelli residences in Latvia and provide the master architect with another vast project.

The old childless Duke of Courland, Ferdinand, died in June 1737 and with him apparently the Kettlers dynasty. Biron saw the opportunity to succeed to the title and obtained the support of the Polish King August III. He also needed to be elected by Courland's nobility and managed to overcome their objections through the payment of large sums smuggled into the country in the form of bills payable in Amsterdam. Work was immediately begun on the main residence, a palace in the capital Jelgava on a site next to the River Lielupe.

Jelgava is 19 miles (30km) northwest of Rundale and Rastrelli was like a horseman riding astride two horses. The foundation stone of the new 300 room Baroque Palace was laid in June 1738. Although exterior work at Rundale was slowed down, the interior was unaffected. Reports on the progress of both buildings were regularly sent every fortnight to the Duke Biron.

Within two years the fortunes of Duke Biron changed dramatically. The Empress died on 28th October 1740. During her last days she ensured that Duke Biron would remain in a powerful position by appointing him regent to the baby Tsarevich Ivan. The son of her niece, Anna Leopoldovna he became Ivan VI against the superior claims of her cousin Tsarevna Elizabeth. According to a contemporary, Lady Rondeau, whose husband Sir Claudius was the British Ambassador at her court, the Empress was a grim, sullen woman and openly sensual. She was a true friend as indeed is shown by her treatment of the Duke, and in her cheerful moments, an amiable companion.

Rastrelli returned to continue his work of reconstruction of both palaces. Rundale was completed in the mid-1760s and the palace at Jelgava in 1772. Duke Biron abdicated in 1769 in preference of his son Peter, and died three years later in the Jelgava Palace, where his body is interred in a copper sarcophagus. Only recently, it was discovered that Ernest Biron was the illegitimate son of the last Kettler, who had an affair with his mother Katharina.

When Catherine the Great annexed Courland, she gave Rundale to Count

Biron's Exile

The duke's regency was short-lived. Three weeks later he was seized in his bedroom at midnight by a rival, Field Marshall Münnich. This was Tsarevna Elizabeth's revenge. Early the next year, when he came to trial and was condemned to death by quartering, the sentence was commuted to exile at Pelym in Siberia. All his property was confiscated including his diamonds, which alone were worth £600,000. Almost twenty-two years later, he was pardoned by Peter III, but it was Catherine the Great, who restored him to his former position in Courland.

The Gold Hall, most luxurious room in the palace

Valerian Zubov and later it was passed on to his brother, Prince Platon Zubov. After his death in 1822 his widow married Count Schuvalov and their descendants held it until 1920.

The house of Courland still exists and Prince Ernst Johann, who was born in 1940, is the current head and lives in Munich.

Tour of Rundale

The approach to the magnificent palace is over the canal bridge and through the semi-circular stables which were designed by both Rastrelli and the Duke's court architect, Severin Jensen. His distinctive trademark, maroon, was applied to most of his buildings although thankfully this is not the case with the gates with their lions, which he also designed.

For some reason the director has maintained fine sand underfoot in the courtyard, so it is preferable to wear sneakers rather than fine footwear on your visit, but this irritant is soon forgotten when you step up wooden stairs into the palace. Inside it is magical and the grand staircase takes you up to the Duke's living quarters and staterooms if you turn left, or to the Duchess' suite and dining room if you turn right.

Out of the 138 rooms, 42 are beautifully restored with period furniture and to the original interiors. Unlike other public buildings, you are allowed behind the scenes to see staterooms in the process of being decorated. (This is a risky business because there are potential dangers on the uneven surfaces and visitors should exercise great care in these rooms.)

The ground floor has the palace kitchens, part of which is a restaurant and part houses the museum. There is a hodgepodge of over 700 exhibits on display in the museum including furniture, paintings, sculptures, textiles, porcelain, glass and bronze covering the Gothic to the Art Nouveau period. An unusual item is a silver goblet owned by Peter, the Duke of Courland, which is inlaid with coins of the mid-1700s.

The pièce de résistance in the palace is found on the upper galleries. In the central building there is a series of rooms leading to the Duke's bedroom which contains two floor-to-ceiling stoves decorated in Delft blue tiles made in Danzig by the potter, Gottried Kater. The twenty interconnecting rooms run in parallel enfilades with a library at one end and a billiard room at the other. The Duke's private chambers run to two studies, a dressing room and bathing room.

The east wing contains the various reception rooms such as the Gold or Throne Room which is the most luxuriously decorated room in the palace with gilt stucco on artificial marble and has definite echoes of the War and Peace saloon at Versailles, and the Gold Gallery of Charlottenburg in Berlin. A surprising feature is the delicate Porcelain Cabinet.

The Grand Gallery, which served as the courtiers' meeting place, links the Gold Hall to the White Hall where balls were held and are still today, as it can be hired for special events. The latter can be described as a paean to whiteness, and it does not take much imagination to see how the resplendent ballgowns stood out as the women dancers swirled by. It also has a porcelain cabinet attached in an oval shape and the vases and jars are arranged to resemble a cascade of water. If anything, these rooms are a living celebration to the great talents of the Prussian sculptor Graff and the Italian painters Francesco Martini and Carlo Zucchi.

The Duchess' apartments in the west wing are simpler and smaller than the Duke's. An outstanding feature is the divan niche in the form of an enormous shell, designed by Graff, in her boudoir.

Around Rundale

The nearest town is **Bauska** which is worth a visit because of its castle and can be reached by car in an hour or hour and a half by a regular bus service from Riga. I suggest you combine this with a visit to the Neo-Classic **Mezotne Manor House**, owned by the von Lieven and situated a short distance away. It has a brilliant rotunda and is open daily from 9am to 5pm, ☎ 392 8921 or 392 8796, Fax 392 8984. A descendant of the family who lived there until 1920 is Anatol Lieven, Russian Correspondent of the Times.

Rastrelli fans may consider a visit to the **Jelgava Palace**, which houses the tombs of the Dukes of Courland. The Baroque building is a shadow of its former glory and is now run by the Latvian University of Agriculture. The Jensen maroon dominates brightly against the white outside. Some twenty-one sarcophagi rest in the crypt including Ernst Johann and his father Duke Ferdinand. Open Monday to Friday 10am to 5pm, ☎ 302 5329.

North of Riga

Hieronymous, Karl Friedrich, Baron von Munchausen (1720-97) of Bodenwerder in Hanover had served in the Russian army against the Turks and when he retired to his estates around Dunte, he would amuse himself and his cronies by relating extraordinary stories of his deeds as a soldier and hunter. He became famous in literary history because of his amusing, mendacious, anecdotes, known as *The Adventures of Baron Munchausen.*

An author, Rudolf Erich Raspe, down on his luck in London, and who had met the Baron, collected them in a shilling book of forty-nine pages which was published in London in 1785. No copy of the book, known as *Baron Munchausen's Narrative of his Marvellous Travels and Campaigns in Russia*, exists but a second edition was printed in Oxford in 1786. A bookseller named Kearsley, brought out an enlarged edition later that year with illustrations under the title of *Gulliver Revived: the Singular Travels, Campaigns, Voyages and Sporting Adventures of Baron Munchausen*; as he re-lates them over a bottle when surrounded by his friends.

There were seven English editions as Munchausen increased in popularity and the book was translated into many languages. A sequel appeared in 1792, dedicated to James Bruce, an African explorer whose book, *Travels to Discover The Nile*, was held to ridicule and incredulity. In time, additions were made by book-seller's hacks and suggestions were taken from Baron Toff's Memoirs, the aeronautical feats of Montgolfier and any topical subject such as Bruce's

The Araisi Lake Fortress

Above: Aerial view of the Zeppelin hangers of the Central Market near the station

Left: An aerial view of Rundale Palace & Gardens

Exhibits in the Palace Museum

explorations in Africa.

Munchausen, as we know it, is a medley of material from all ages, from Lucian's Vera Historia and Renaissance Facetiae to contemporary travels, real and imaginary.

The country house in Dunte is no longer there but an old pond where

Places to Visit

Munchausen Museum
Dunte Vidzeme
7.5 miles (12km) north of Saulkrasti
☎ (40) 20333, (40) 20107
Open 10am to 6pm Wednesday to Sunday. Closed Monday/Tuesday.

Bicycle Museum
44a Riga Street, Saulkrasti
You can also take in a bicycle museum with thirty restored machines including a Dutch penny-farthing.

Cepli ceramic workshop
☎ 923 4867
Before the Dunte-1 sign on the right off the Riga-Tallinn road. A selection of milk pitchers, vases, mugs and bowls are on sale and the kiln is in the potter's backyard. Ingrida Zagata has been casting pottery for the past fifteen years.

Araisi Lake Fortress
Cesis Region, Drabesis, LV-4140.
☎ 419 7288/7293
Open 10am to 6pm, May 1 to October 15.

he caught five ducks at once with a piece of bacon tied to a thread can be seen. The Munchausen Museum is sparse on exhibits and includes two pairs of old hunting boots, the afore-said stuffed ducks strung across the ceiling, animal trophies on the wall and a sled.

Although the Baron is out of fashion today his name has been used to describe a bogus medical condition, Munchausen Syndrome. The patient simulates different medical conditions on a regular basis to gain attention even to the extent of undergoing surgical operations. This can also occur when a parent makes a child ill or pretends they are ill and requests medical attention, Munchausen's Syndrome by proxy. Such a situation can happen often and the child recovers when separated from the parent.

The most interesting place is the pub next to the museum which has good traditional Latvian cuisine and is open every day from 10am to 9pm. There are bonuses to visiting his museum. There are the wild beaches of Saulkrasti (sunny shore in Latvian) where you can swim and which can vary from sand with high dunes and stony beaches to meadow beaches where grass grows to the water's edge.

The Araisi Lake Fortress

A window to the past life of Latvia's largest tribe the Lat-gallians during the late Iron Age (ninth to tenth century BC) is shown at a castle built on a sandbank in the middle of the lake. There was a local legend of a fortress, the **Araisi lake fortress**, sunk in the lake and it was only in 1965-1969 when archaeological excavations were carried out that this was found to be true. The dig was difficult as the water level had to be lowered 3ft (1m) and dykes had to be built around the excavation trenches. Nevertheless, water seeped through and had to be pumped out.

Several interesting aspects were revealed about the Latgallians. An archaic form of house construction was used unlike any other found in building. These were single log cabins with sloping roofs, covered with strips of spruce or birch bark inside rather than ceilings and an annexe, the sleeping quarters, was attached to the right of the entrance. The door frames were rather low indicating short people who also had to be agile to walk on the round surfaces of the log platforms.

Each house had a clay floor with benches along the walls. There were ovens and shelves for cooking utensils and sculptural figures of the inhabitants dressed in their clothes. Necklaces, bracelets and remnants of clothes were found as well as ancient tools, like narrow bladed axes, chisels and wooden wedges, with which the buildings are being reconstructed.

The whole complex of over twenty houses was surrounded by high walls and the archaeologists were surprised to discover that the island was not a natural formation but purpose-built.

The concept of a fortress surrounded by water is not new, as a similar arrangement was still in existence in the sixteenth century in Mexico City. The Aztec capital during Montezuma II's time, which was on a grand scale compared to Araisi, was built on a lake and could only be reached by a causeway which had a series of bridges to allow sea traffic past.

The Conquistadors had to fight hard to conquer the city, as it was well protected by the surrounding water and only one causeway which could easily be defended. There were also fleets of canoes which could bring in supplies in the case of a siege and attack anyone who appeared on the causeway. The Latgallians would have had a similar stronghold in the middle of the lake when attacked by the Vikings. In a country which has some 4,000 lakes, water fortresses would have been popular and could have provided adequate protection from enemies and wild animals.

The Araisi lake fortress is the only Iron Age site in Latvia and the first in north-east Europe to be extensively studied. There are other attractions, a fourteenth-century church and castle which is in ruins.

5. Culture

Opposite: At the Opera in Riga

Little is known about Latvian literature as few works have been translated into English and on my visits I was fortunate to meet a poet and two authors. Like other states under Soviet occupation, a systematic attempt was made to eradicate their culture. But this was not a new situation as it had occurred before under other rulers and champions have always risen among the people to defend their heritage.

The literary scene

When the German Barons had sneered at the peasant lifestyle in nineteenth century Krisjanis Barons rose to the challenge and produced his encyclopaedia of Dainas, a six-volume collection of songs. (See entry, Dainas). In the last century, Janis Rainis, issued a figurative call to arms and defend the Latvian identity with the publication in 1905 of the verse collection *Vetras Seja (Seeding of The Storm)*. But this was a subtle force, without violence or bloodshed, that swept the country stimulating a new thinking and consciousness.

Mara Zalite, editor and publisher at *Karogs* magazine, was another figure from the literary establishment to voice her concerns at a meeting in the Riga Philharmonic Auditorium to commemorate those who died during the Stalinist purges. 'We have been made to feel like exiles in our homeland. We have been expelled from our spiritual birthplace. Banished from our way of life, driven from our farmlands. Torn away from our culture – severed from our folklore! Separated from our songs – cast out of our language! Driven from Europe – exiled from civilisation!'

She was unaware at that time that freedom was only a stone's throw away, for a year later independence was declared again, the second occasion in the twentieth century.

I was met at the Salapils station by Knuts Skujenieks, one of the country's foremost poets and translators. We walked for half a mile (1km) along a dusty and broken pavement, towards his house in a quiet cul-de-sac, where I was going to spend a night.

Once I had settled into my room, Knuts and his wife, Inta, a botanist who cultivates their large vegetable garden at the back of their house, welcomed me with a drink of vodka and a meal. 'It is a special' he said of the vodka. 'I bought it as it comes from Jelgava, the town where your father was born'. I was touched.

Knuts was proud to show me his study, which was a light and compact room at the top of an open staircase.

Rainis and Aspazija

Rianis and Aspazija were the golden couple of literature at the beginning of the 20th century. They both were succesful poets and playwrights and played important roles in the 'New Current" democratic movement that championed independence from Czarist rule. When the Latvians showed solidarity with the Russian revolutionaries during 1905, Rainis fled the country with a 10,000 ruble reward on his head and his wife, Aspazija, followed him into his Swiss exile where they remained for 15 years until the First Latvian Independence. It was a most productive period for Rainis and one of his ballads, Daugava, spurred on the troops during the First World War to win a decisive battle over the Germans that led to their freedom.

They returned to a hero's welcome in 1920 and he was elected to parliament and held several government posts until his death in 1929.

Theirs is also fascinating love story and an account of their life together as well as the period in exile is given in the book, Borders published by Neputns. (See page....)

The shelves were chock-full with his translated works from over thirty languages and several volumes of his poetry.

Our conversation was wide ranging from eighteenth century history to Dainas and analysis of Latvia's psyche. He told me about the Lutheran clergyman Ernst Glück who lived in Aluksne and made the first translation of the Bible into Latvian. When the town was captured by the Russians in 1702, he and his family, including his child's nurse Marta Skrovronska, a Lithuanian, were taken prisoner.

It was this selfsame woman who became Catherine I. Taken to St Petersburg she first became the mistress of Prince Menshchikov a friend of Tsar Peter the Great and, then the Tsar's consort and wife. Another interesting fact about Aluksne, which I learnt later, is that the author of *The Leopard*, Guiseppe de Lampedusa, lived there in the Manor House in the 1930s.

For him, the Dainas are marvels because in only four lines there are unlimited possibilities of expression. The perfect square of two lines about nature and two about human life allows this. His most preferred is the one about the godfather, which is a symbol of the sun.

'Dear Godfather
what will you do
when all of us die?
Who will give you the
bread in your old age?'

Before we part the next day, I ask him about the Latvian society since Independence. 'There are many hang-ups' he said 'We are masters of our destiny yet we still think with a slave's mentality. We lack initiative to solve problems and still think we will find the answers through an executive body.

There are still many who suffer from self-pity. They complain we're small, we've been oppressed and are dying out as a nation.

When I returned to Riga I knew I had been with a sage because however many questions I asked him, he was always ready to give me a considered, incisive opinion. During our discussion on Dainas, he immediately suggested that I meet the world authority, Dr Vaira Vike-Freiberga, and he rang her up so I could make an appointment to see her. I did and within a month, I heard she had been elected president. Later, I found that the mention of his name to others was equivalent to a letter of introduction.

Andrea Neiburga is quite different. She considers herself as being part of the second generation of writers, the first was under the Soviets who always toed the line, for them criticism meant ostracism, exile and possible death. When I was told about her brilliant collection of short stories and expressed an interest in meeting her, the secretary of the Writer's Union suggested I make an appointment through her secretary. I was impressed as I thought she had landed a fat advance and begun a spending splurge because she is one of the few Latvian authors whose work has been published in English.

As we sat in Osiris, one of the in-places in Riga, she disabused me of my notions. She had stopped writing since independence and the secretary that has been referred to, helped her run the family's real estate business.This is a loss, as she was particularly well known for her satirical style. She wrote of the annihilation of the human ego felt during the collapse of the Soviet Empire.

'My generation was very shocking about reality' she said 'and there were a lot of opportunities to sell stories. Now it is hard to make a living from writing. That's why I am in business'. She points to others from the third generation, Paul Bankovskis whose most well-liked author is Roddy Doyle and Janis Einfields, originator of the super-short story. They are in the vanguard of experimental writing. The others have fallen silent.There is little now to challenge and no government line to espouse. Social realism is dead.

The Writer's Union has also fallen on hard times. They formerly occupied a mansion belonging to the Benjamin family situated in the middle of the city, and when it was recently returned to the owners, the Union moved to small, new premises out in the suburbs. Knuts Skujenieks welcomes this new era. 'I prefer the dirty, tiring prose of every day life' he said after he had won another of his innumerable awards.'The fact that we can tramp around the base of the Freedom monument, yelling and screaming, or say what we think of our president... ha! ha!'

Now that is something to write about but first the latter day Philip Roths or John Updikes must get under the skin of the cult of individualism.

Pushkin's Love in Riga

In the churchyard of the former St Peter and St Paul Church which is now the Ave Sol concert hall, there is an unusual monument, a sculpture of the head of an attractive woman, Anna Kern, who inspired Russia's greatest poet.

She was born in 1800 in the Orel province where her grand-father, I P Wolf, was the Governor. But her parents moved to Tversk, 93 miles (150km) north-west of Moscow where she grew up. At the age of sixteen she was married off against her will to a fifty-two year-old, General Ermolay Kern, who had impressed her parents with the prospect of making a good match.

As a couple they were a total disaster as he was a professional soldier, having been promoted through the ranks and caring only about the army. She had artistic aspirations, had read widely during her youth and acted in amateur theatricals. Her husband was coarse and she abhorred him. She lived the life of an army wife, moving from town to town and bore him two daughters. Life was tiresome as her husband was either asleep, on army duties or smoking. She complained that she had 'not a single soul to talk to' and her head spun from all the reading.

A notable event in these early years was a meeting with Tsar Alexander during manoeuvres in Riga in 1817. He found her attractive and invited her to visit him in St Petersburg. She declined, but asked the Tsar to come to Lubny, where they were stationed. He laughed off her suggestion.

In 1824, when she returned to her parent's estate, she was given copies of Pushkin's poems, along with the first chapter of Eugene Onegin, by Arkady Rodzyanko who lived next door.

On another visit from Riga a year later, this time to her aunt, Praskovya Alexandrovna Osipov-Wolf, she met the poet who had been exiled to his father's estate, Mikhailovskoe, because of his involvement with the Decembrists. He appeared during lunch carrying a tall stout stick, which, according to Anna Petrovna, was his usual habit. He usually ate earlier and would be accompanied on his visit by two large wolfhounds.

When he was introduced to her, he said nothing. He tended to avoid the people living in the vacinity who became butts of his satire in Eugene Onegin. However, the Osipov-Wolfs who lived at Trigorskoe were an exception as he enjoyed their company and large library. Unpredictable in his manner, he showed a full range of emotions when he was there from noisy exuberance, bouts of depression, shyness and sadness.

'Incapable of hiding his feelings', Anna Petrovna said, 'he always expressed them sincerely and was indescribably good when something pleasant excited him. When he decided to be friendly, nothing could compare with the sparkle, the wit and attractiveness of his speech.'

They saw each other daily and the night before she left her aunt suggested that they paid a visit to Mikhailovskoe. They set off in two carriages: Pushkin, Anna Petrovna and her cousin Anna Wolf were in one and her aunt and son, Alexey Wolf, in another. 'Never before or afterwards did I see him so kind and cheerful' she remarked. 'He joked without sarcasm and sharpness, praising the moon without calling it stupid.'

They did not go into the wooden house, which Pushkin called his hut or izba, but went to the old, overgrown park. There they walked down an avenue of lime trees and he recalled their meeting six years earlier before he left St Petersburg. But seeing her again had rekindled tender feelings and inspired one of his finest love poems, I Remember the Wondrous Moment.

The next day before she set off for Riga with her cousin, Pushkin arrived with a copy of chapter two of Eugene Onegin. He had also written a poem for her and hidden it in one of the uncut pages. It was the love poem:

'I remember the wondrous moment
You stood before me
Like a radiant fleeting dream
A vision of perfect beauty'

And after four verses it concluded:

'Once again my heart is filled with elation
It's excited and delighted
and awake to inspiration
Awake to life, love and tears'

She read it and when she wanted to place it in her casket, he had second thoughts and snatched it back. Later she repeated the lines to his great friend Baron Anton Delvig who printed them in his magazine, Northern Flowers and to Glinka who set them to music.

Pushkin was in the throes of a crush on her and wrote to her cousin in Latvia. He told Anna Wolf 'every night I roam the park and repeat to myself "she was here". The stone on which she stumbled lies on my desk, beside a branch of fading heliotrope'. Another missive was also sent off to the aunt. But the longing for her became hard to bear and soon, on 25th July, he wrote directly to her asking whether she would agree to correspond with him, and happily she did.

'A correspondence leads to nothing, I know; but I do not have the strength

(cont'd overleaf)

(cont'd from previous page)

Pushkin's Love in Riga

to resist the desire to have a word from your pretty hand', he writes frankly. Then he struck a Byronic pose in the second part of the letter. 'I take up my pen again because I am dying of boredom and I can't get you off my mind'. Next he sensed the danger of an affair with a married woman which excited him. 'I hope you will read this letter in secret… will you hide it again in your bosom? If you fear my indiscretion... Sign with a fictitious name, my heart will be able to recognise you'. One can imagine Anna Petrovna walking along Citadel Street, Riga and smiling to herself about the affair, her secret secure in her bosom.

The family was housed in the officer's quarters adjacent to the Barracks in the square. Sometimes, she may have entered St Peter and St Paul Church and lit a candle for the Almighty to bless their love.

Pushkin had been exiled by Tsar Alexander I for six years and he would have chafed at the thought that he could not go to Riga when his romance with Anna Petrovna turned into passionate love. His mother wrote an emotional letter to the Tsar on his behalf requesting permission for him to travel to Riga to consult a specialist there, purportedly for his varicose veins. It was refused.

She returned in October to Trigorskoe with her husband and the lovers managed to be alone several times. They discussed plans for her to separate from her husband and hints of this appeared in one of his letters to her. 'This is the fine project which has plagued my imagination for the last quarter of an hour. Yet imagine what would be my happiness. You will say: "But the explosion, the scandal?" What the devil! Upon leaving a husband the scandal is complete, the rest is of no consequence'.

After her short visit, he referred to her in another missive as 'an angel fate sends to delight my solitude'. When he later discovered that she had been also corresponding with Alexey, in a fit of pique and jealousy he dismissed her as 'our whore of Babylon' in a letter written to him later.

A year later she left her husband and went to live with her father in St Petersburg in the same house as Delvig. On some occasions she carried out errands for Pushkin, who was still confined to Mikhailovskoe, and once sent him a book of Byron's that he had requested. Not much of their correspondence survived from that period except a letter which she had written jointly with her cousin, Anna Wolf. 'Anna Petrovna Kern orders me to tell you that she is selflessly delighted by your success… and loves you sincerely, with guile'.

She was present on his nameday in 1827 which was celebrated with his family. When a friend remarked that she had not given him a gift in

return for his poems, she took off her mother's ring and put it on his finger. He promised to match her gesture and the next day gave her a ring with three diamonds.

There is always the question of whether their love was ever consummated. Evidence is provided in a reply to a letter from a friend 'Falstaff' Sokolevsky, who worked in the Department of Foreign Affairs. 'You don't write me anything about the 2,100 roubles I owe you!' he wrote, 'but you write me about Mme Kern, whom with God's help a few days ago I fucked'.

There were other amours after Anna Petrovna until he married Natalya Ivanovna Goncharova. Incidently another Tsar, Nicholas I, took a fancy to her and it is likely that she succumbed to his charms. The Tsar later made provision for her and the children after Pushkin's death.

The woman who came from Riga was the one he immortalized as a vision of perfect beauty. In the Pushkin museum in St Petersburg, there is a copy of the poem that she transcribed, as well as a good imitation of his signature which she signed for her scrapbook. She is buried on a small estate, Mitino, in the family graveyard some six versts (4 miles/6.4km) from Torzok. There is also a Pushkin museum in the old trading town dedicated to his travels in the Tver region where he had stayed with his many friends on their small country estates. Strangely enough he had done sketches of the park and the graveyard too.

Although Pushkin never managed to see Riga, there are strong associations with the city because the descendants of his closest friend, Delvig, originated from the city and of Anna's presence there.

Velta Snickere

A Latvian poet in exile who has lived in Crouch End, London for almost six decades. She is a metaphysical poet with a small oeuvre.

Gaïa

Horses and cows wrinkle their skins
To skake off
bothersome insects
How long will earth
Tolerate humanity

From the collection Husks, Libraire-Galerie Racine, Paris

For Ram
You said we were two halves
Of one sea star
Before there was land.
And every time we meet
Grief touches deep
Homesickness

Nora Ikstena

Is one of the most interesting writers in Latvia today but little of her work has been translated into English except for a few extracts in some literary magazines and an essay about Rainis in Borders (see pages…….). She has written 10 novels, short story collections and biographies and has a rich heritage of Russian literature – she was born under the Soviet occupation of her country and could read her favourite authors, Bulgakov, Dostoevsky, Ysenin and Anna Akhmatova in the original, and English literature. After her language degree at the University of Latvia, she took a postgraduate course in English at Columbia University, Missouri. There her teacher was Dzintars Sodums, who had undertaken a lifelong work of translating Joyce's Ulysses into Latvian, and she was familiar with the work in both languages.

Her work which uses structural binarisms and alternates from everyday events described in her engaging, spare style to stream-of-consciousness passages of sex and violence, can be ranked alongside Angela Carter. Her heroines are women like Arija Kalveks who was born in Kalvi farm and marries the callow and insecure George (Gogis) Fetzer in Riga's Dom Cathedral (Arija flies across lake Alogs).

'It's all very quick with Gogis. For her it's no more than an unpleasant moment of bracing herself. When all they used to do is kiss, she'd tingle, throb and flush all over. She'd thought that come the day she could really bite the fruit, hanging so fragrant and juicy in front of her, it would burst, drip, run down her chin, her throat, right down into her navel. It wasn't like that. They kissed for a nice long time, but then Gogis began to rut like a pig at the trough, and once he gained access, he moved three times, accompanied by a rather loud voice, and then felt back in utter ecstacy. She was amazed by his rolled-up eyes. Maybe the smell of fruit is all women get? On a visit to Kalvi, Arija confided in Milda (her mother), asking for advice. Milda was sewing towels with her sewing machine and nearly poked her finger with the needle:

"If your flower isn't properly plucked, you'll have to go and get separated up!"

She has had a love-hate relationship with Rainis, the 'Latvian Shakespeare',

which began when, as an impoverished student, she worked on his correspondence. She had had branded him a neurotic because of his compulsive hoarding of every scrap of paper. However, in revisiting his place of exile, Castagnola, Switzerland, she was able to appreciate the process of creation, the border between the dream world and reality.

Dainas – songs

Like the ancient Greeks, Latvians have a strong oral tradition, but theirs has not been in epics like Homer's Odyssey and Iliad which originally were sung, but in folk songs. They focus on nature, on the panoply of Gods, on human relationships, on the seasons and life, and earlier ones on the Sun like the Ancient Egyptians. Essentially, they are philosophical and have provided wisdom for the Latvians over thousands of years.

It is as unique to the Latvians as *haiku* is to the Japanese. The first two lines of the quatrain present an image from nature, the last ones echo with a parallel from human life.

An example:

'The meadow is beautiful
but it is most beautiful when it is ploughed
A bride's wreath is beautiful
But most beautiful is a married woman's hat'

The Dainas were classified according to several major themes. One cycle followed the stages of human life from the cradle to the grave with the attendant family feasts and rituals of which weddings were most numerous. A second followed the solar year with seasonal festivals and celebrations, mid-summer songs being the most popular. A third significant category is devoted to work songs while a fourth is about singing itself. In addition there are mythological magic spells, children's, and erotic songs.

The Academy of Sciences in Riga has logged over three million songs, which is the largest collection in the world. An assiduous compiler, Krisjanis Barons, who was a mathematician and astronomer, published six volumes of almost 182,000 song texts between 1894 and 1915 at the time when the country was run by the German minority and ruled by Russia. A nationalist, he had been provoked by the German Barons who intimated that the Latvians could not have a culture as they were peasants. The encyclopaedia of Dainas was his answer. The task took him three decades and was begun by meticulously filing bits of paper in shoeboxes and later transferring them into seventy drawers of specific size to contain them in a special custom built cabinet.

Dr Vaira Vike-Freiberga, the President of Latvia, is the world's leading authority and exponent of the Latvian Dainas. For her each of the songs represents a poem. 'They are implosions of creativity within the confines of strict metric frameworks' she says. 'On the surface the Dainas speak of apparently mundane, concrete things; yet the concrete is but a vehicle for a deeper abstract idea. The Dainas do not depict concrete reality, they transfigure it. It is the verbal alchemy that takes the common metal of all that the singer encounters and transmutes it into

Cont'd on p120

A detailed look at the Dainas

The first song in the enormous collection of Krisjanis Barons was:
'One girls sings in Riga
Another sings in Valmeira
Both sing the same song.
Could they be daughters of the
same mother?'

Most of the songs are quatrains and their lyrical quality derives from the fact that they are never objective descriptions presented by a detached narrator. They are live testimonials from active participants cast in the first person of the lyrical 'I'. The singers are often transposed into the roles suggested by the lyrics. Take the following examples:

'Why, o sun, did you tarry
Why did you not rise earlier?
I was delayed behind the hill
Warming the little orphans'

A third couplet can be added:

'I warmed hands, feet
I dried off their tears.
The swan swims
on the river.
I swim among other people's gossip'

A simple interpretation of the swan's song is that a girl's reputation is sullied through gossip and her repartee is that as water does not cling to a swan's feathers, nor will the ill remarks of others cling to her.

The four-line strophe is the fundamental building block of the huge edifice of the folk song corpus.

The Dainas, mostly, do not refer to specific people like Lize or Milda or Mikus or Peteris. They are universal, referring to the eternal bride, mother, father, bridegroom, brothers, or sisters.

'A bright star came down
By the door of my bride
That was not a bright star
That was new born child's soul'

The major periods of human life are marked off through successive rites of passage including marriage, funeral rights and the comings and goings of the seasons.

'Black ravens are crouching
At my graves edge
These were not black ravens
Relatives stand crying'

Like other cultures, there are examples for the archetypal mother-in-law, who

(cont'd overleaf)

is a pain in the butt.

'Not every morning the sun rises
With red little rays
Not every day my mother-in-law
Was good to me'
Or
'I heard in the kitchen lean-to
Fir logs spluttering
That was not fir wood
That was the son's mother'

Trees in the Latvian language have association with the different sexes. Thus ozols (oak), osis (ash), vitols (willow) and berzs (birch) are male, while liepa (linden), ieva (bird cherry tree) and abele (apple tree) represent the female. The Latvian abele is a word of ancient Indo-European origin since the stem is known in at least three Baltic languages.

There are further distinctions with tree types as an apple tree is motherly, a linden is a young girl and a bird cherry tree is frequently a wife or a bride. The oak on the other hand, represents three kinds of males; boys, men or husbands.

The fourth volume of Barons' Dainas contains an entire section about woods and trees and 20 different kinds are mentioned. Apple is the fruit of love according to the linguist Velta Ruke-Dravina and 'is easily discerned in the erotic songs of the sixth volume of Latvian Dainas where a woman's breasts as well as male genitals are compared with apples.

In sexual songs the motif about 'driving the little horse through the apple grove' has the same meaning as 'I gave the rose garden to the little horse to harrow'. There are associations too with the Greek myths where the apple is also a symbol of love and fertility.

Of special interest to Dr Freiberga, is the cycle of Sun songs of which there are some 4,500 texts. Sun or Saule (pronounced sowleh in Latvian) is a feminine noun and appears in songs as a beautiful female figure. It is the mythological and divine being that is being conjured up. When an orphan girl marries, the sun a generous godmother enriches her plain wool cloak with gold shining floss.

A significant task of the setting sun is to bring along with her the souls of all those mortals who have been laid to rest in the earth on the preceding day.

'My dear mother has left
Along with the sun
I called out, but she couldn't hear
I ran after her but in vain'

There is the lovely physical aspect as the sun is the celestial timepiece, with its sunrises and sunsets and in the heralding of the seasons. This is framed in the Dainas, but again repeatedly, one finds the philosophical:

'What shall I earn
While living in this sun?
Two sheets of white linen
A room of four planks'

Or as Goddess or God-like figure

'Dear White Saule in your course
Please 'even out' this earth
The rich are quite ready
To bury the poor alive'

The Latvian pantheon is filled with divine personages to rival the Greeks, the Romans or the ancient Egyptians. Laima is a version of Athena for she can take a human form and appear amongst people. She determines the fate of mortals as is shown:

'As Laima cast my life
So must I live it
I cannot go counter
To dear Laimas decree'

Or

'Rise early, my Laima dear
Be late in retiring
Help me to lighten
My life's heavy burdens'

Mara, who is looked upon today as Mother Latvia, is closely linked to cows. She is invoked during childbirth and like her counterpart in Egyptian mythology, Hathor, she is a mother of heaven. Janis, which means the Johns, has a dual role echoing the two-faced Roman God. He is the force of attraction between male and female and also plays the Dionysian role during the midsummer night feast. The equivalent of Jupiter in this heavenly firmament is Dievs, which originates from the Indo-European word, 'The bright Sky'.

'Higher sings the lark
Than any other bird
Dievs holds wise council
Over the whole of the world'

One of the aspects of virtue; tikums' is to respect Dievs, to 'hold' him as the Dainas put it. This does not mean humbling oneself before him or them. When someone suffers ill fortune, or is oppressed, the Dievs or Laima will 'lift them up' and restore their self-respect.

Tikums consists of several desirable character traits. A lack of virtue is not cause for a feeling of guilt but for shame and the price is ridicule and ostracism.

Teacher's recollections

He was a perfectionist' Kapralis said 'and serious. When the class had free time, Misha would go into a corner and reherse over and over again'. But there are other qualities which a dancer must possess, besides a big talent. According to his teacher, 'You must be phys-ically strong, a good actor, an excellent partner who pro-vides stability and strength, be good at jumps and turns, and above all, have a good tech-nique'. He gives the example of the Nutcracker. 'Misha, who played the toy soldier, would always think of his role. I was dancing as the prince, when the mouse king died, I noticed that Misha relaxed his body'. When he was asked why he had done this, he replied 'When Mouse King dies, toys become human. Toys become boys and must change'. I was impressed because even as a small boy he had devised that himself'.

poetic gold.'

The recorded song texts are a pale shadow of what a song would have been when it was sung. 'Live' songs accompanied by a melody occur in a specific social context. They are aimed at an audience, be it a baby in a cradle, a festive crowd such as a wedding, Midsummer Night celebration (Jani) or the singer themselves while they are grinding grain on a handmill.

According to Dr Freiburga this largest single repository of published and oral folklore is a rich seam of the ancient Latvian way of life revealing the daily tasks, cares, joys, sorrow, beliefs, customs and values of the people. There are echoes of an old cosmogony, a mythology and a social order, and they take on a breadth and scope that acquires an epic quality.

Without a doubt this oral tradition of songs serves as a cultural history of the Latvians. But some claim it is more for it has gathered and documented a people's way of life, their philosophy, moral code and aesthetic judgement and as such should be considered to be like the Old Testament.

Latvians are indebted to Barons who has returned their unique heritage to them through constructing a vast verbal monument. It is the first time in the history of mankind that an unbroken cultural record exists of a nation over thousands of years. The fact that it is still relevant today demonstrates its flexibility and resilience. As such, it should be looked upon as a gift to the West, which is on a par with anything that the Greeks or the Romans gave, but unlike the Latvians, they have vanished.

The final word should be given to Dr Freiberga who puts the Dainas into their present context. 'The Dainas allow us to reconstruct a metaphysics in which the highest aim of a human life is to live in harmony with the will of the gods, with the rhythms of nature, and with other members of society' she says. 'Personal worth and integrity are expressed in terms of possessing virtue, not in terms of avoiding sin, which is a concept alien to the Dainas. The basis of personal virtue rests on reverence for the gods, respect for one's elders, and the indefatigable ability to work hard all one's life.'

This sounds like a perfect viewpoint for the twenty-first century.

Since 1873, traditional song festivals have been held every five years. The last festival occurred in 1998 and took place in Mezaparks. Some 20,000 singers and dancers participated over a week.

Ballet

Riga School has had its fair share of top ballet dancers such as Maris Liepa and his son Andris, John Markovsky and Vladimir Gilvan but it has also produced one of the greatest stars this century – Mikhail Baryshnikov. The school is situated opposite the old town across the river in the suburb of Pardaugava although in a new building. His teacher, Juris Kapralis is still on the staff coaching future stars.

Mikhail Baryshnikov was born in Riga in 1948 after his father, Nikolas, an Air Force officer was sent to the city as a lecturer in military topography. It was a second marriage for both parents and his mother Alexandra brought along Vladimir his stepbrother who was eight years old. Mikhail had little in common with his father, a cold, curt man and more with his mother who was interested in culture. She would always take Misha along when she went to the theatre, opera or ballet.

As a boy Misha had 'ants in his pants' and could never sit still. When Alexandra became friends with a ballerina from the Bolshoi Ballet in Moscow who gave ballet lessons, she enrolled him in the classes. He was nine years old and she felt he could channel his energy into dance. It was a good decision as Misha had a talent for expressing himself in movement.

'I got lucky,' he said. 'I fell in love with dance'. Two years later he was accepted at the state ballet academy, the School of Chor-eography, and was put in Juris Kapralis's class together with Alexander Godunov who became a friend. 'Even as a small boy he was very musical' said Kapralis, 'but he also had the huge possibility for hard work.'

An event occurred in Misha's life which although tragic gave him the impetus to develop his talent. He had gone on a visit to his grandmother who lived on the Volga river outside Gorky. For some reason his mother returned to Riga earlier. She hanged herself in the bathroom of the communal flat. She was found by Vladimir and his father was loath to talk to him about it. It was a traumatic experience as he admits he was 'mamma's boy'.

When his father got married a year later, Misha understood that he was no longer welcome and began to lead a peripatetic existence. He stayed with other families for periods and then the ballet school would ring them up and warn them that they should send Misha home otherwise they would have to call the police. He went through all the problems of teenagers and worried about his height. He believed he was too short to be a ballet dancer and slept on a wooden plank to grow faster. He was fortunate that Kapralis had a sunny disposition and was a brilliant teacher, so Misha thrived, not least because he was a child workaholic.

When Baryshnikov reflects on this difficult period he is not bitter. 'Human

At the opera in Riga

beings are extraordinarily powerful survivors' he said 'When you lose your parents it is a fact of life'. He was grateful though that his mother did not commit suicide in front of him. Although he never had a serious relationship with his father he does not blame him as he feels he is responsible for all the difficulties in his own life.

In 1964, the Latvian State Ballet went on a tour of St Petersburg and the teenager Baryshnikov went with the company in a small role. During the visit he met Alexander Pushkin, a teacher, at the Kirov Ballet School and was asked to join the class. Kapralis was proud of this and when he asked after Misha later he was told by the Russian, 'Please give me more pupils like Baryshnikov'. There are three great ballet dancers of the twentieth century according to Kapralis, Nijinsky, Nureyev and Baryshnikov.

'He was fortunate' said Kapralis, 'because he gained an intellectual approach to ballet from us as opposed to the Russian School which is strong on bravado and can at times be mannered. Here he learnt acting, good form and good line'.

Kapralis has a superb reputation for nurturing talent and one of his new stars is a twenty-one year-old Pavel Vasilchenko. He met Baryshnikov on his last visit to Riga two years ago and is still impressed with his former student. 'Now he dances in another way', he said, 'Modern dance is easiest when you are older. But he is still number one for his age'.

Mikhail Baryshnikov defected to the West in 1974 and is now living in the US directing an American modern dance company, the White Oak Dance Project. Alexander Godunov is a principal dancer in the company.

The Riga School of Choreography is at 10/12 Kalnciema Street, ☎ 761 5870.

Music

'Music is the most cultivated of the fine arts. A good operatic company, and five singing clubs are among the amusements of Riga', The John Murray Handbook for Travellers in Russia, Poland and Finland, 1865.

Music has been one of the oldest forms of culture as Latvian songs date back to time immemorial *(see entry Dainas)*. The songs gained recognition when the first song festival was held in 1873 and was followed by Krisjanis Barons' encyclopaedia of Dainas, which was completed in 1915.

Richard Wagner

Even before that, Riga was firmly established on the provincial music circuit and Richard Wagner was one of the first eminent musicians to have engagements in the city from 1837 to 1839. In fact he was desperate to come to the city 'I am breadless' he wrote to his friend Louis Schindelmeisser from his sister Ottilie's house in Dresden 'I must get Riga'.

When the director of the theatre, Karl von Holtei, offered him the post, he travelled by sea, which was cheaper than the land journey from Lubeck, at the end of August via Travemunde, where he had to wait for a week for an agreeable wind. He took lodgings a few minutes from the theatre in

Schmiedestrasse and found that his qualifications for the job had been his supposed interest in light French and Italian music which was popular with the patrons.

However, the composer did not tell Holtei that he was undergoing a change of heart and had gained a dislike for such musical trivialities. His emotional problems with his wife Minna, he contemplated divorce, and his dire financial circumstances had no doubt contributed to this state. There were other sources of irritation; the stage, the orchestra, the theatre, the company which was incomplete and the small audiences, only 3,000 patrons out of a population of 70,000.

While he was in the city he managed to arrange a temporary position for his sister-in-law Amalie Planer a singer, and at the same time became reconciled with his wife Minna. She and Amalie arrived in Riga on 19th October 1837. Soon the trio moved to more spacious accommodation occupying the top of a house at the corner of Dzirnavu and Brivibas streets.

It was large and consisted of a salon with windows overlooking each street, a bedroom for the couple, two rooms for Amalie and Wagner's study with a divan, a hired grand piano and a desk on which he wrote the first two acts of *Rieuzi*. People living nearby remembered Wagner sitting at an open window smoking a pipe and dressed in a dressing gown with a Turkish fez on his head.

Minna had made the ill-founded decision not to work, and they decided to live on Wagner's scant income. There was speculation that the decision was due to Wagner's jealousy. She flirted with the theatre patrons and there is a suggestion that she had an affair during her marriage.

He set about his task as musical director with energy, zeal and perfection, which was normal for his theatre work. Fifteen operas were rehearsed and produced during the first year and twenty-four in the second. He was an unforgiving taskmaster, a role that did not please the company, as nothing was good enough or finely shaded for him. There were endless rehearsals and soon complaints and grievances from the singers and members of the orchestra were commonplace.

Matters were not helped by the fact that Wagner was antisocial, he did not

Musical visitors

Other musicians such as Anton Rubinstein, Robert Schumann and Klara Wieck, before she married Schumann, Franz Liszt, and Hector Berlioz followed in his wake and the tradition has con-tinued into the twentieth century when Bruno Walter, Benjamin Britten, Otto Klemperer and Carlos Kleiber visited the city. Dimitri Shostakovich also found a haven here after he had fallen into disgrace with Stalin and his works were no longer performed. The opera, Lady Macbeth of Mzensk was premiered in Riga in 1946 and conducted by Edgars Tons.

disguise his distaste for fun-loving, empty-headed audiences or the bland repertoire. A further offence was that he refused to write incidental music for the theatre director's mediocre plays. And he also set a new tradition for conductors, for he no longer faced the audience during a performance. He turned his back on them.

Although Minna was slightly ill when she arrived she was easy to live with because of her repentant attitude and her desire to please her husband. However, his peace was disturbed when Amalie was replaced by another singer, and in her disappointment began to quarrel with her sister. Soon they no longer spoke to each other.

It was a matter of time before Wagner was in debt and his financial position became known at the theatre. Although he was living on a knife-edge he was undergoing inner development which made him indifferent to his outside world. He had enemies at the theatre, no friends in the town and his one consolation was that his work on *Rienzi,* on which he had pinned his hopes for material success in Paris, was progressing well.

In a letter written to Theodor Apel after his departure of this period he said with a trace of irony; 'I obtained a good and respectable post as music director in Riga. There I spent two fairly tranquil years; I might almost say that there I began to feel myself again but for the fact that it became ever clearer to me that I am not built to earn my

bread in this way. I sought stupefaction in the almost frenzied performance of my duties; but my body was not fitted for this, the northern climate being trying for me'.

By March 1839, the crunch had come, his unpopularity with the performers and overwhelming debts, which if payment was enforced by the creditors could land him in prison, forced the hand of the theatre committee and he was dismissed. As the dismissal only came into effect in the summer, they also laid plans for his flight from the city.

Wagner was furious when he was sacked and railed against Heinrich Dorn, a friend who had been appointed to replace him. 'I had a serious illness, a nervous fever threatened my very life. Hardly had I begun to recover when I heard that during my illness my seeming friend Dorn had dis-placed me in the most perfidious manner' he wrote to Apel in the same letter.

To escape from Latvia which was part of Russia was no easy task because the frontier was well guarded and anyone proposing to leave the country had to advertise their intention in the local newspaper, in the event of creditors having a claim on them.

When the company went to Mitau, as Jelgava was then known, Wagner decided to leave the country there, where he was unknown. By arrangement he and Minna were smuggled over the border to Prussia as contraband goods by Polish Jews. Robber, a huge Newfoundland dog owned by a local Riga merchant, that had taken a liking to Wagner, accompanied them.

They were taken to Pillau in Prussia and not Konigsberg, which was nearer, because he was on the creditors wanted list there too. From there they sailed

The composer Richard Wagner

to Paris, the focal point of the operatic world, and to fame and fortune. He did not conquer Paris and had to wait another three years before *Rienzi* brought him that success he had hoped for in Dresden.

The Riga period, on hindsight, was seminal as he was inspired to begin a sketch of the *Flying Dutchman* on his voyage from Pillau. Because of stormy weather this had taken three weeks instead of eight days. Wagner had matured sufficiently to shed his illusions and develop his artistic ambitions that would result in the Ring.

He left his mark on the city too. Most of the opera audience at the time were unaware of his importance and were astonished at his later fame, but were generous enough to name the theatre

Opera House

after him as well as the street where it is located.

After Wagner

The interesting question is whether anyone of Wagner's stature has emerged since. Jazeps Vitols (1865-1948), founder of the Latvian Academy of Music is considered one of the country's greatest composers. He was a teacher at the St Petersburg conservatory and friend of Nikolai Rimsky-Korsakov. Most of his contemporaries like Melngailis trained at St Petersburg as the new generation would study at the Latvian State Conservatoire of Music. The two main contenders for the slot of top composer appear to be Imants Kalnins and Peteris Vasks.

Straight away, I must mention that it is hard to make a living from composing classical music in Latvia, let alone anywhere else in the world, and that Imants Kalnins is also an MP. He had several brushes with the Soviet regime and their tough tactics, so that later when the country achieved independence, the exercise of political power appealed to him and he became a member of parliament.

He recalled an occasion when an official from the Union of Composers told him he could not perform a new oratorio *The Poet and the Mermaid.* The story is about a sea sprite and a poet who longs to follow her to a new world.

'I still remember the woman in the office, she was not belligerent or rude, she simply shook her head and said "No, we can't allow this to be performed". When asked why she smiled, "These two lives, they're too mystical, I can't quite understand these two lives". I asked her maybe you think it represents capitalist life and socialist life. She grinned at me "I don't know, but you can't perform it".'

'Everything was politics', he said 'Every word. Even your smile. It was jail, a real jail'.

His interests as a composer are wide and his oeuvre includes rock and pop music, a passion that began in the sixties when he toured with his rock band. He enjoyed star status and when a popular folk-rock band Menuets who performed Kalnins' compositions were banned he came to their aid. The oppression stopped when they added his name to their list of songwriters.

'But there's also this patriotic element to his music as well' said Imants Mezaraups of the Medins Music College in Riga who highlights his mass appeal, 'Its typical for Latvians to break out with folk songs in the middle of dinner parties, including Kalnins' songs'.

Indeed his work is closely identified with the symbol of resistance during Soviet times and his symphonic pop fourth symphony was performed on the seventy-ninth anniversary of Independence on 18th November 1997.

Peteris Vasks who was born in 1946 and is five years younger than Kalnins was never attracted to political power. On the contrary he has resisted politics with every fibre of his being. Of his work Cello Concerto, which was dedicated to the celist David Geringas and completed in 1994, he made a strong statement about his position.

'I wanted to tell in music of the persistence of a personality against crude brutal power', he said 'About sources of strength which helped us to endure it all. What totalitarian power did to us. How we are to purge ourselves from the man-ipulation. Above all, how we are to carry on with our lives'.

When he wrote the *Book* for solo cello in 1978 he was asked about the inclusion of the wordless human voice. 'An important factor in my music', he explained 'has always been spirituality and protest against power. I wrote mainly instrumental music, which did not come under KGB control. They could control literature and cinema but they could not understand instrumental music!'

In Latvia, he is considered to be a serious composer whose work is appreciated abroad. He is also not popular with the mainstream like Kalnins 'I write music not for the mass of people but for the individual' he stated firmly.

I was keen to know what the international music scene thought about him and talked to Yakov Kreizberg a young and brilliant conductor who was born in St Petersburg where he was a music prodigy, before he emigrated to the US when he was sixteen. He is

New influences

Vasks was not allowed to study in Riga as Kalnins did, because his father was a Baptist minister and was forced instead to go to the nearby Lithuania's State Music Academy. The only Latvian composer of his generation to do so, he came under unusual influences like the avant-garde Polish music of Witold Lutoslawski, which made a memorable impression on him. He studied ancient music, classical drama and mastered technicalities of twentieth century works of Schoenberg, Webern and Berg.

Unlike Kalnins who won accolades under the Russian regime – winner of the All-Union Competition of Young Composers in 1969, State Prize winner in 1977 and Peoples Artist of the Latvia Socialist Soviet Republic in 1985 – Vasks abhorred political hack work.

He points out the positive aspects of that period. 'Under the Soviets, concerts meant more here as people listened attentively to the undercurrent of spiritual protest in the music' he said. 'This unified the musicians and the audience. Of course you don't want the iron curtain back, but in such an atmosphere music is very important to people'.

an outspoken musician, who is chief conductor of the Komische Opera in Berlin and of the Bournemouth Symphony Orchestra, who persuaded the BBC to commission a piece from Vasks for the 1999 Promenade concert.

He was first introduced to Vasks through David Geringas who when they did a concert together played the music for his encore. 'It was stunningly beautiful' he said of the *Book* for cello 'That got me interested in Vasks. Later when I bought the first CD which featured the euphonious *Cantabile for Strings*, I thought it was terrific and now the work is part of my standard repertoire.'

The *Book* had a similarly powerful effect on an indie label producer. John Kehoe who heard it on the car radio was to produce several CDs on Conifer.

Soon Kreizberg also wanted a new work from Vasks because of its reflection of the twentieth century and its conflicts. He wanted the composer to break out of his small world of the chamber orchestra. He did this with the Second Symphony which was premiered in the Royal Albert Hall, London and was Vasks' first large scale work. 'It was like a child who had a few toys to play with being let loose in the toyshop' was how Kreizberg described the experience.

If he was to place him in the music constellation, Kreizberg is adamant that he is a major figure whose works are deeply Russian in the richness and depth of the melody. There are certain gestures which you would find in Shosta-kovich for example. But then

Russian heritage

When Kreizberg was asked whether he still considered himself Russian, he answered with great honesty 'My understanding of Russian music, literature and culture is in the blood'. He also explained how to play Shostakovich's music because the wrong tempo radical changes the effect.

'When I hear Shostakovich's music' he said, 'My bones ache' – it was the only way he could express his pain, his anger and contempt. 'I'm not saying non-Russians can't do it justice but they don't auto-matically know what lies behind it. 'If you play the first movement of the Fifteenth Symphony at a brisk tempo, as some do, it becomes perky, a parody, like a joke. If you play it slightly slower it becomes scary and menacing and that's the way I believe he meant it. It's the same with the finale of the Fifth Symphony. It doesn't take much to make a difference between it sounding triumphant or evil. That's typical of Shostakovich'.

again the Second Symphony sounds very English because of the strong presence of nature besides the bird sounds.

'It's music of our time' he said 'The composer is committed to nature and deeply religious whether you believe in animism or God, and there are the brutal conflicts of the twentieth century reflected in it too'.

Andrejs Zagars

Andrejs Zagars, General Manager of the Latvian National Opera, is a latter-day Diaghalev and Balanchine all wrapped up in one. There is the impresario who wants to create fresh new productions quickly, and who wheels and deals with money and people. Then there is the artist who wants to nurture (audzinat) young talent, to train them and to push them to excel. Take for example *Eugene Onegin*, which I saw and discussed with him afterwards. It was first staged in Riga over a century ago in 1896 and was sung in German but this time it was in the original Russian.

For the stage director,Victurs Kairiss, it was only his third production and a risk to Zagars. 'I had to trust him' he says 'and usually I'm saved by my intuition'.

In this instance he is right. Kairiss succeeds in balancing the ironical man with 'a young woman with an open soul whose ideal is love... and then comes an arrogant... attractive male who possesses a strong masculine aura and demonic strength and provokes in Tatyana emotions incomprehensible to her'. Her possession is shown in wild bedroom scenes where she feverishly writes letters on the bed and sees his image on the mirror, which is used to brilliant affect as a projection screen.

The other memorable scene is the

duel, which occurs at a height on a narrow bridge.

The overall effect is not tired or stale but exciting. It is not unusual therefore that he is packing in the audiences and during his brief reign of about three years he has increased attendances from sixty-three per cent to an enviable eight-six per cent, figures that the current Chairman of Covent Garden would no doubt goggle at. Another amazing fact is that Zagars does this for the same amount as it takes to keep say Sir David Frost in Havana's a month – $300.

Unlike other artists before him, Nureyev and Baryshnikov, who dreamt of escaping to the West, there was no Margot Fonteyn or Gelsey Kirkland respectively, into whose arms he could fall. The big question in his mind was could he live in any other country than Latvia?

During Independence he decided to travel in Europe and the USA and live abroad. After two years in exile he believed he was too homesick and returned. He still acted in both films and the theatre, but decided to change his career. He became a restaurateur. 'In Soviet times, bars and restaurants were in dark cellars' he says 'as people didn't want to be seen and wanted to talk in secret.'

In 1993, he opened the Black and White Bar which was decorated in a minimalist, modern style that has now become his trademark. Six years later he is hailed as the Latvian 'Conran' with four restaurants, a bar and a wine shop. He goes by the dictum less is more and a visit to one of his places bears that out as you will find cool, clean, modernism reminiscent of Conran's Butlers Wharf.

It was his love of food and interior design that brought him back into the theatrical world of musical drama. 'My soul is happy when I'm running something and not being a slave of a bad director'.

There were many problems at the Riga Opera House and one day he got a call from the Prime Minister, Andris Skele. 'He told me that he wanted someone to kick ass and asked whether I was willing!' This was the way the offer was put to Zagars. The house had become a laughing stock amongst the Latvians, and a butt of jokes, as it was being managed by a wealthy timber merchant who had been brought in because of his business acumen. But he was no match for the Soviet style administration and he and the productions floundered like a fish on land.

Zagars had the right qualifications with the appropriate commercial experience, a creative background, and was ready for a challenge. He had new ideas that he was impatient to put in to practice, and not afraid of taking on the old truculent establishment. The opera scene world-wide is known for its intransigence, particularly in the face of reform and many houses, like Paris have seen off potential saviours or creative Czars. The Latvian Company was no different and he immediately ran into a fight when he decided to join as General Manager.

He shrugs off those days with 'I'm used to being in stormy waters, but the difference was that I was not the Captain of a small boat but a huge tanker which takes time to turn. I'm in

Andrejs Zagars' early life

Andrejs Zagars is without doubt a fascinating fellow. Before opera, he was a matinee idol in Soviet films. With his clear-cut handsome looks and non-Slovak features, he played foreigners and I wager that if he had been born in the West he might have ended up playing Superman or a Rambo-like character in Hollywood. He is over 6ft (1.8m) tall, fit and his personal dynamism makes him welcomed to any group.

He was born in Siberia of Latvian parents and when they returned to their homeland in 1959 he studied mathematics and physics. There was an inevitable draw to the theatre and movies and in his short film career, he has appeared in fifteen pictures. His main roles were playing heroes and he eventually tired of this, 'In my soul' he says 'I felt uncomfor-table' The best film he acted in was Good Luck Gentlemen, which was directed by the famous Russian director, Bortko. This is the only one in which he does not win the girl in the end.

He was happier in the theatre and some of the productions he played in include Eugene O'Neils' Long Days Journey into Night, Shakespeare's Romeo and Juliet as Mercutio and Goldoni's Servant of Two Masters.

charge of 610 employees, and responsible for everything'. His mission was clear. He would create the best singers and musicians, the best opera house in the Baltics and eventually in Europe.

Such talk did not appeal to some of the incumbents who were selfishly interested in maintaining the status quo, even if it meant blocking other younger and talented singers, musicians and dancers. The fight turned ugly and some members even resorted to voodoo, sticking pins into the costumes of their rivals. 'At times I felt I was in the trenches' he muses 'and the only loyal person I had was my assistant who joined with me'. In the end, there were three casualties and Zagars had won the war.

The climate was good – the artistic levels were high and he could build on the tradition of excellence. He was also inspired by the newly renovated Riga Opera House that was built in the 1860s. 'I wanted to ensure that the art here was worthy of such a magnificent building'.

Zagars does not bemoan the fact that he is not heavily financed like the eighty opera houses in Germany. 'When society gets state funding there is a tendency to become complacent' he observes. The productions are usually led by stars and produce boring performances in which there is no story, little acting and none of the components blend together. Such a situation, in his eyes, is wrong. 'Opera is a drug for me, not the stars. I want to make it a moving experience so by the

Fulfilled mission

He was now able to carry out his mission statement of the best opera and gave major roles to talented young singers like Sonora Vaice and Inga Kalna. They have fulfilled his prediction of brilliance and have received acclaim in Austria and the United Kingdom. Placido Domingo raves about Sonora and has performed with her on many occa-sions. She has brought star quality to the title role of Handel's Alcina. Inga Kalna is another discovery who has found a perfect role as the Countess in Mozart's Marriage of Figaro. Another newcomer who has come out of the Zagars stable is the young conductor Andris Veismanis. Already, there are several Latvian international stars, the likes of Maris Janson, Inessa Galante, Egils Silins (Guesting at the Met) Gidon Kremer and Misha Maisky. The quality of the orchestra's strings is worth commenting on as it has produced the latter two stars.

end of the evening you are transformed. We achieve that once or twice a year, *Aida* is one example'.

Opera economics is blighted by the star system that results in high ticket prices which limits the audience to an elite.The people who come to the performances in Riga are a cross-section of the public and the prices are low in comparison to other houses. The General Manager's target is to get a full house on each occasion to ensure future interest in this art form. Educational programs are being developed to understand good art and the opera.

The LNO with its 1,100 seats is certainly worth a visit and the restaurant, which is situated under it and was once a resonator to contribute to its perfect acoustics, will not disappoint. Every year in June, there is a special festival.

Accommodation in Riga

Hotels:

Luxury

Europa Royale Riga

60 rooms

12 K. Barona iela,

☎ 7079444

fax 707 9449

riga@europaroyale.com

www.hoteleuropa.lv.

New hotel, housed in a restored 19th century splendid mansion that once belonged to the wealthy Benjamin family. It overlooks Vermanes garden. All rooms are different in size and colour with high stucco decorated ceilings and have restored parquet floors and modern air conditioning. The house, which is an architectural monument, has kept all its authentic design elements. The lobby bar and restaurant make an elegant and impressive meeting venue.

Grand Palace Hotel

56 rooms

12 Pils iela

☎ 7044000

fax 7044001

www.grandpalace@schlossle-hotels.com

www.schlossle-hotels.com

Prices include breakfast.

Located in the Old Town, the rooms are decorated in the English and French Classicism style and offer all facilities including those for the handicapped, anti-allergy rooms, business centre, and a health club. The hotel also has two elegant restaurants – Orangerie and Seasons.

Hotel Bergs

38 rooms

(in Berga Bazars) 83/85 Elizabetes iela,

☎ 7770900

fax 7770940,

reservation@hotelbergs.lv

www.hotelbergs.lv

Prices include use of fitness centre with sauna and gym facilities. There is also wheelchair access and parking available.

For a hotel with ultra chic credentials, there is only one address in Riga, Hotel Bergs. This is an establishment that pampers guests during their stay with spacious rooms, discrete and efficient service and a gourmet restaurant. The architect, Zaiga Gaile, has set the tone of cool throughout with her light and dark, wood and linen minimalist interiors. In the lobby lounges, dark African furniture and sculptures blend well with the white background and in the Club room, where guests can relax with a cognac, internet or chess, three portraits of the Berg women, including one by the illustrious Rozentals (see page…), hang on the walls.

All the rooms which offer modern facilities such as climate control, high-speed internet access, as well as a kitchen or wet bar, feature Studija Naturals elegant designs of linen bed covers and curtains (See pages…) and are decorated with Ilmars Blumbergs paintings.(See pages…) The loft and penthouse suites are unique as they are designed to be split-level with the bedroom on the upper level. The penthouse suites have terraces and balconies where in summer guests can sun themselves. Bergs is crowned by an unmatched architectural element - the stunning glass enclosed rooftop conference room that provides the ideal setting for business meetings, special receptions and banquets. The comfortable lounges and fitness centre also provide a good place to unwind. It is an ideal spot for a long stay because when guests do stir, they have even have a trendy shopping centre, Berga Bazars on their doorstep.

Hotel De Rome

88 rooms, 18 suites and 1 apartment

28 Kalku iela,

☎ 7087600

fax 7087606,

reservation@derome.lv

www.derome.lv.

Prices include breakfast and the use of sauna. Parking lot available.

It is situated in one of the best sites in Riga, at the edge of the Old Town near the Opera, city park and the Freedom monument with embassies, shopping and business centres a short walk away. There is a central atrium with luxurious rooms on several floors. A popular spot for celebrities including Paul Young, Nick Cave, Mariss Jansons, Mikhael Barishnikov and royalty such as the Queen of the Netherlands. Ideal for businessmen as there are facilities for seminars and conference rooms with a maximum capacity of 100. The restaurant Otto Schwarz on the top floor of the hotel is the place for power breakfasts and the Romas Operas Galerija bar for a night-cap.

Reval Hotel Ridzene

95 rooms, 3 suites and 1 apartment
1 Reimersa iela,
☎ 7772345
fax 7772332
latvija.sales@revalhotels.com
www.revalhotels.com.
Prices include breakfast, underground parking and use of the fitness centre. All facilities have wheelchair access.

This deluxe hotel is located within walking distance of nearby embassies and overlooks two of the city's main parks. State-of-the-art facilities for leisure and fitness centre where you can enjoy a marvellous panoramic view from the sauna. It was a former hotel for the Soviet elite Complement your stay with fine dining at the Piramida restaurant.

SAS-Radisson Daugava

361 rooms, 44 suites and 53 junior suites
24 Kugu
☎ 7061111
fax 7061100
riga@radissonsas.com
www.riga.radissonsas.com
A popular global brand it is situated on the wrong side of the river but the lack of an ideal location is compensated by a splendid view of the Old Town's medieval skyline.Good business facilities with a fitness centre and a large swimming pool.

Upmarket

Ainavas Boutique hotel

22 rooms, 3suites, 5 junior suites and 1 apartment
23 Peldu iela
☎ 7814316
fax 7814317
reservations@ainavas.lv
www.ainavas.lv.
Prices include breakfast buffet. This boutique hotel is located in the Old Town in a medieval building. Each guest room is individually decorated and has a photograph of a Latvian landscape (ainava) above the bed; includes down duvets, plush bathrobes and bottled spring water. There is a fireplace in the 15th century lobby bar and an inner courtyard.

Gutenbergs

38 rooms, 1 suite and 5 junior suites
1 Doma laukums,
☎ 7814090
fax 7503326
hotel@gutenbergs.lv
www.gutenbergs.lv.
Situated in the Dome Square of the Old Town. The rooms are small but very comfortable, equipped with cable TV, internet access, safety deposit and other amenities. There is a penthouse restaurant with a good view of the square. Also offers well-equipped conference facilities.

Monika Centrum Hotels

80 rooms, (3 suites, 50 doubles, 12 singles, 14 junior suites and 1 apartment)
21 Elizabetes,
☎ 7031906
fax 7031912
monika@centrumhotels.com
www.centrumhotels.com.
Elegant hotel situated in the prestigious Art Nouveau district of Riga, housed in a renovated splendid 19th century Neo-Gothic style building. The lobby boasts Italian marble floors and a fireplace. Many rooms have balconies with views of the park. Suites have four-poster beds.

Boutique Hotel 'Viesturs'
13 rooms and 1 suite
5 Mucenieku iela
☎ 7356060
fax 7356061
info@hotelviesturs.lv
reservation@hotelviesturs.lv, www.hotelviesturs.lv.
Located on a quiet side cobbled street of the Old Town in a restored 17th century building. It has an intimate atmosphere and the rooms are quite small with country-inspired bathrooms that feature wash basins with flower designs. A feature is the winding staircase with its ancient exposed stone walls. The prize room is the suite which has a private rooftop terrace with a magnificent view, as well as a bathroom equipped with a sauna and a Jacuzzi.

Konventa Seta hotel
141 rooms and apartments
9/11 Kaleju iela
☎ 7087501
fax 7087515
reservation@konventa.lv
The hotel is a unique complex of 9 medieval buildings and is situated on the original site of a 13th century convent. The well-run hotel offers all the modern conveniences in its rooms and has conference and banqueting facilities. It is popular amongst musicians including Gideon Kremer. There is also a well-appoined restaurant, Raibais Balodis, and bar Melnais Balodis in the ho☎ Within the restored courtyards, there are a variety of shops, bars, museums and an open-air café.

Centra Hotel
27 rooms, 5 suites and 5 junior suites
1 Audeju iela
☎ 7226441
fax 7503281
hotel@centra.lv
www.centra.lv
Prices include buffet breakfast.
A minimalist hotel which is located in the Old Town. All rooms have a varied décor and the ones situated on the third and fourth floors have high ceilings. The hotel is on the doorstep of popular pubs and offers a good view of St Peter's and St John's Church. Conference room available.

Moderate

Forums

32 rooms and 3 junior suites
45 Valnu iela,
☎ 7814680
fax 7814682,
reservation@hotelforums.lv
www.hotelforums.lv
Located in the Old Town, the hotel offers comfortable double and triple rooms, suites with sauna or Jacuzzi and some with balconies. It is within walking distance of the tram and bus stations.

Karavella

80 rooms (58 doubles, 12 singles, 4 suites and 6 junior suites)
27 Katrinas dambis
☎ 7323130
fax 7830187
hotel@karavella.lv
www.karavella.lv
Parking lot. The 3-star hotel is in the port area and not too far from the centre. In a high-rise building, it is value for money. Ask for a room with a view.

Kolonna

41 rooms (18 doubles, 2 singles, 8 triples, 2 suites, 11junior suites)
7/9 Tirgonu iela
☎ 7358254
reservationriga@kolonna.com
www.ho☎kolonna.com.
Located in Old Riga, near the Dome square, this new non-frills hotel has satellite tv and WiFi. The rooms have good views and breakfast is served at the trendy Emihls Gustavs chocolatiers on the ground floor.

Inexpensive

Enkurs

17 rooms (14 doubles, 2 singles and 1 suite)
87 Caka iela
☎ 7846340
fax 7846339
info@hotelenkurs.lv
reservation@hotelenkurs.lv
www.hotelenkurs.lv.
The hotel is located in the centre of Riga, in one of the busiest main streets of the city.

Sampetera Maja

22 Apuzes iela
☎ 25925871
☎ 26030869.
Parking. This guesthouse is located on the way to airport, approximately 5 minutes from Riga Centre and Old Town. Jacuzzi, sauna, fridge, microwave oven, air conditioning are also available.

Viktorija

43 rooms (24 doubles, 10 singles, 1 triple, 3 suites, 5 junior suits)
55 Caka iela
☎ 7014111
fax 7014140
Parking. Located on one of the major shopping streets, the hotel occupies an old Art Nouveau building.

Vilmaja

49 double rooms
12 Ilmajas iela
☎ 7873222
fax 7872778
reservation@vilmaja.lv
www.vilmaja.lv.
Prices include breakfast and parking lot. Situated in a residential area. Sauna available.

Bed and Breakfast

B&B Riga

43 Gertrudes iela
☎ 7278505
mob. ☎ 26526400
home@bb-riga.lv
www.bb-riga.lv.
Family run bed & breakfast situated in a quiet courtyard in the historical centre. Cable tv and a laundry service available.

KB

37 K. Barona iela
☎ 7312323
fax 7316953
hotel@kbho☎lv
www.kbho☎lv.
Located 10 minutes away from the Old Town, all rooms have cable TV.

Lenz

2 Lencu iela
☎ 7333343
mob. ☎ 26302222
fax 7331378
pasts@lenz.lv.
Price includes breakfast and airport transfer.

Accommodation in Jurmala

Jurmala, the seaside and spa resort of Riga is some 15 miles (24km) from the middle of the city. Trains, buses and taxis provide a good service into Riga and many visitors prefer to stay here during the hot summer months.

Hotels:

Moderate

Baltic Beach Hotel

165 rooms and apartments
Majori, Juras 23/25
☎ 7771400
fax 7771410
info@balticbeach.lv
www.baltic-beach.lv
The hotel offers a spa and resort centre including a swimming pool with seawater and a fitness centre.The A wing has luxurious doubles, suites and apartments with balconies and sea views. The C wing offers the same facilities without seaviews and the B wing has rooms with Soviet style furnishings. The spa centre is state-of-the-art and the restaurant is one of the best in Jurmala. The hotel is located on the beach.

Concordia

14 rooms
Majori, Konkordijas 64
☎ 979 49 45
fax 753 63 63
hotel_concordia@ho☎com
www.concordia.lv
Completely renovated, the hotel is only a ten-minute's away from Jurmala's bustling pedestrian street, Jomas iela. The staff can also organise spa treatments.

Hotel Eiropa

40 rooms
Majori, Juras iela 56
☎ 776 2211
fax 776 22 99
hotel@eiropaho☎lv

www.eiropahotel.lv
The hotel located by the beach and is spread over three buildings. All guests can use the gym and sauna, a playroom is available for children and babysitters can also be arranged. In the summer barbecues are held in the palm garden, but you can also sample delicious European cuisine in its award-winning restaurant.

Hotel Jurmala Spa

190 rooms
Majori, Jomas 47/49
☎ 778 44 00
fax 778 44 11
www.hoteljurmala.com
The modern hotel and spa has 23 massage rooms, two pools and five different types of saunas. Other facilities include a conference centre for 700 people, beauty treatments, a fitness centre, casino and restaurant. The rooms have good views.

Pegasa Pils

37 rooms
Majori, Juras 60
☎ 776 11 49
fax 776 11 69
www.pegaspils.lv
A hotel housed in an historic, renovated Art Nouveau masterpiece built in 1900. The bedroom of the unique bridal suite is located under a chandelier in the main tower of the building. It also has the largest restaurant in Jurmala.

Villa Joma

16 rooms
Jomas 90
☎ 777 19 99
fax 777 19 90
www.villajoma.lv.
The green and yellow building is located at the end the bustling pedestrianised street.An unusual feature is that each guest's breakfast is cooked to order every morning

Lielupe

120 rooms.

Bulduri, 64/68 Bulduri Prospect

☎ 775 2755

Fax 775 2694

Hotel 220yd (200m) from beach with tennis courts, mineral water indoor and outdoor swimming pools and sauna.

Vaivari

80 rooms, 200 rehabilitation rooms.

Vaivari, 61 Asaru Prospect,

☎ 776 6122

Fax 7766314

A spa hotel with mud, thalassotherapy and medical consultations. It s also caters for rehabilitating children.

Jaunkemeri

200 rooms.

Jaunkemeri, 20 Kolkas

☎ 7733242 & 7733522

Fax 773 1889

Situated in the furthermost village from Riga, the spa has a good reputation.

Inexpensive

Jaundubulti Cottages

36 rooms.

Jaundubulti, 59 Dubulti prospect

☎ 776 7045, Fax 7767518

Simple accommodation in apartments including kitchen.

Daina

120 rooms.

Melluzi, 59 Melluzu prospect,

☎ 776 7057 Fax 7767056

Hotel with tennis courts, swimming pool, sauna, and all rooms with balconies. Situated 220yd (200m) from the beach.

Zvaigzne
12 rooms.
23/24 Meierovica prospect
☎ 776 4681
Fax 7764672
A small quiet hotel near the beach.

The Jurmala Spa and
Tourist Centre
Majori, 42 Jomas,
Jurmala LV-2015
☎ 776 4276/776 2167
Fax 776 4672
E-mail jurmalainfo@mail.bkc.lv
A busy helpful office that offers accommodation bookings as well as general tourist information on everything at the seaside.

Climate in Latvia

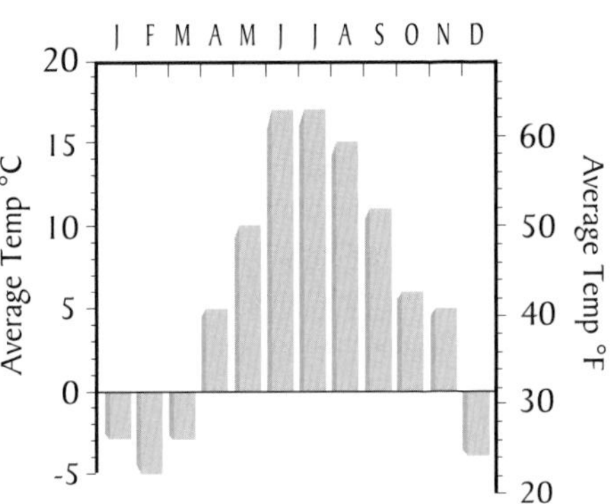

Latvia has a temperate climate, which has considerable temperature variations. Summer is warm with long hours of sunlight, until midnight during the solstice on June 23-24. Autumn and spring weather is mild while winter, which lasts from November to mid-March, can be extremely cold with temperatures below zero. Rain occurs throughout the year with the heaviest in August; snow is usual in winter.

Concert Halls and Opera Houses

Arena Riga
Sporting events and large concerts
13 Skanstes
☎ 738 8200

Ave Sol
Hall of Chamber Music
7 Citadel Street
☎ 702 7570

Dome Cathedral
1 Dome Square

Dzintari Concert Hall
1 Turaidas Street, Jurmala
☎ 776 2092
Fax 776 2086

Great Guild

Concert hall of the Philharmonic Society, 6 Amatu Street
☎ 721 3798

Music Academy

1 K Barons Street
☎ 722 3847

Opera House

Latvian National Opera
3 Aspazijas Boulevard
☎ 707 3777
Fax 722 8930
E-mail boxoffice@opera.lv
Box office open 10am to 7pm.

Riga Congress Hall

5 K Valdemara Street
☎ 732 3370

Riga Latvian Society

13 Merkela Street
☎ 722 6881

St John's Church

7 Jan Street
☎ 722 4028

St Peter's Church

19 Skarnu Street
☎ 722 9426

Small Guild

3/5 Amatu Street
☎ 722 3772/721 0093

Wagner Hall of Chamber Music

4 Richard Wagner Street
☎ 722 7105

Currency

The Latvian currency is the lat, which was introduced in 1993 and has remained stable since that time. The lat is divided into 100 santims, pronounced in a similar way to French centimes. Bank notes come in denominations of 5, 10, 20, 50 100 and 500 lats.

Banking hours are from 9am to 4pm, Monday to Friday. There are currency bureaux throughout the city and most restaurants and shops accept credit cards. Cash point machines are available at banks throughout the city and tourists need never be short of currency. Euro and US dollars are readily acceptable currencies, even by taxi drivers.

Customs Regulations

Items made in Latvia over 50 years ago are subject to a 20% duty, while foreign items made more than 100 years ago face a 10% duty. Subjects from certain European countries are exempt from these taxes.
For more information, contact the Ministry of Culture, 22 Pils,
☎ 721 4100 fax 722 7916. Open 8.30 am to 5 pm.
Closed Saturday and Sunday.

Diplomatic Corp

Australia *(Consulate)*
1-305 Arhitektu
☎ 7224251

Canada
20/22 Baznicas
☎ 781 3945

Ireland *(Consulate)*
21-632 Valdemara
☎ 703 5286
fax703 5323

Israel
2 Elizabetes
☎ 732 0980, Fax 783 01 70

UK
5 Alunána,
☎ 7774700, fax 7774707

USA
7 Raina Bulv.
☎ 703 6200, Fax 782 00 47

Driving Information

Driving is carried out on the right hand side of the road and the speed limit varies from 31mph (50kph) in towns to 60mph (90kph) outside.

On entering Jurmala, all motorists are expected to pay one Lat, which is a car tax. There are no parking meters in the area. Parking in the Old Town of Riga is expensive, five Lats per hour. The roads vary in quality so be careful of potholes. Petrol is cheap.

Electricity

The voltage in Latvia is the standard European 220 volts and if you want to use an electrical appliance you will need an adapter as plugs have twin points.

Facilities for children

Livu Akvaparks (Livonian Aqua park)
36 Vienibas prospect, Jurmala.
1200-2300. Sat and Sun 1200-2200.
Activities include seven sliding tubes, river, swimming pool with artificial tide, a special zone for children, baths and saunas.

Lido Recreation Centre

76 Krasta iela

1100-2100 Amusement park. 1000-2300 Bistro.

☎ 7504420

One of the biggest log cabins in Europe houses several restaurants, a playroom and an amusement park.

Go Planet

2b Gunara Astra iela

☎ 714 6346

The largest and most modern entertainment centres in the Baltic States. Activities include go karting, laser games, movies and special musical performances including a circus for children.

Jurmala Beaches.

Just outside Riga are 32 kilometres of sandy beaches including the blue flag beaches of Majori and Bulduri

Open-Air Ethnographic museum

440 Brivibas iela

1000-1700 daily

☎ 7994510

A display of 16th to 19 century Latvian houses, farmsteads, windmills, wooden churches and fishermen's villages from different regions of the country.(see page...) It is situated in a large pine forest by lake Jugla and over weekends, traditional craftsmen are at work such as blacksmiths and woodcarvers as well as beekeepers.

Flag

The flag originated during a battle between the Latgallians and the Knights of the Sword, in which the Latvians were victorious. Their king was unfortunately seriously wounded and laid to rest on a white sheet. After he died, his followers found that there was a parallel stripe of blood either side of his body, while the area where his body had been was miraculously untouched. They adopted it as their flag.

Flights

Riga is well served by major airlines and the airport (RIX) is only 4 miles (6.4km) from the city.

There are excellent connections from the US and Europe through **Lufthansa** which flies via Frankfurt, **Air Baltic** and **SAS** via Copenhagen and Stockholm, **Finnair** via Helsinki, **British Airways** via Heathrow, **Austrian Airlines** and **Lauda Air** via Vienna.

Airport (Lidosta)

Useful numbers

Information ☎ 720 7009/722 3305

2nd Floor (Book rooms for some hotels including airport Latavio Hotel, Russian style 8-11L)

Lost property	☎ 720 7236
Passenger Service	☎ 720 7935
Customs	☎ 720 7043, Cargo ☎ 720 7503
Immigration	☎ 720 7208
VIP Lounge	☎ 720 7132, Fax 720 7257

Airport Transfer

There are taxis as well as a regular bus service, number 22, from the Airport to the middle of the city. It only costs 18 santims and the journey takes about half an hour. The time taken by taxi is about 20 minutes and costs about 10 lats.

Riga Information (Arrivals level) ☎ 720 7800, Fax 720 7100. Also can provide accommodation.

Airline Offices

Aer Lingus

I-2, Kalku 11a
☎ 735 77 36
www.aerlingus.com
Open 09.00-18.00. Closed Sat, Sun.

Aeroflot

B-4 Gertrudes 10/12 – 18
☎ 778 07 70.
Fax 778 07 71
rixtosu@aeroflot.ru
www.aeroflot.lv.
Open 09:00-17:00.
Closed Sat, Sun.

Air France

KLM Royal Dutch Airlines Airport,
☎: 766 86 00
fax 766 82 07
reservations.baltics@klm.com
www.kim.lv
Open 05:30-17:00, Sat, Sun 05:30-13:00.

AirBaltic Airport

☎ 720 77 77
fax 720 75 05
reservations@airbaltic.lv
www.airbaltic.lv.
Open 05:00-20:00, Mon, Fri 05:00-19:00, Sat 05:00-18:30, Sun 05:00-21:00. Also on C-4, Elizabetes 85a (Berga Bazars), ☎ 720 77 77, fax 722 42 82. open 09:00-18:00. Closed Sat, Sun.

Austrian Airlines Airport

☎ 750 77 00
fax 750 77 01
office.rix@aua.com
www.aua.com
Open 09:00-17:30, Sat, Sun, 13:30-16:30.

British Airways Airport

☎ 732 67 37/720 70 97
fax 720 71 10
www.britishairways.com
Open 11:00-17:00.
Closed Sat, Sun.

CSA Airport

☎ 720 76 36/720 79 36
fax 720 73 37
www.czech-airlines.com
Open 05:30-17:00, Fri 09:00-17:00, Sun 05:30-15:30.
Closed Sat.

EasyJet

www.easyjet.com
Easyjet offers cheap direct flights between Riga and Berlin (Schonefeld).

Estonian Air Airport

☎ 720 70 69
fax 720 75 05
www.estonian-air.ee.
Estonian Air is represented by airBaltic at the airport. Open 05:30-20:00, Sat 05:30-18:00, Sun 05:30-23:00.

Finnair Airport

☎ 720 70 10
fax 720 77 55
www.finair.lv
Open 09:00-17:30, Sat, Sun 09:30-13:00

LOT (Polish Airlines) Airport

☎ 720 71 13
fax 720 72 13
ilzelot@latent.lv
www.lot.com.
Open 09:00-17:00, Sat, Sun 12:30-15:30.

Lufthansa Airport

☎ 750 77 11, fax 750 77 13
riga.Lufthansa@dlh.de
www.lufthansa.lv
Open 09:00-17:00, Sat, Sun 11:00-15:00.

Norwegian

www.norwegian.no.
Norway's low cost airline now offers cheap direct flights between Riga and Oslo.

Ryanair

www.ryanair.com
Europe's leading budget airline now offers cheap direct flights between Riga and Dublin, Frankfurt (Hahn), Glasgow (Prestwick), Liverpool, London (Stansted), Stockholm (Skavsta), and Tampere.

SN Brussels Airlines

Matisa 30
☎ 784 64 30
sn@gofly.lv
www.gofly.lv
Open 09:30-18:30

Turkish Airlines Airport

☎ 735 94 44
www.thy.com
Open 09:30-17:00, Sat, Sun 12:30-17:00.

Uzbekistan Airways

B-3 Elizabetes 11
☎ 732 45 63
www.uzairways.com
Open 09:00-18:00, Fri 09:00-17:00. Closed Sat, Sun.

Health

There are no reciprocal health agreements between the EU, UK or US, therefore medical and/or travel insurance is essential. No health certificates are required when visiting the country.

Internet Information

Latvian Web

Welcome to Latvia
www.lv

Museums of Latvia

vip.latnet.lv/LMA/
A site that has information on over 100 museums in Latvia. All are members of the Latvian Museum Association.

Hotels in Latvia

www.itl.rtu.lv/CM/hotels.html
Information on many Latvian hotels with photos. Some hotels have on-line booking forms to book a room in advance.

Latvian Centre for Contemporary Art

www.camp.lv
This is a museum for contemporary art on internet.

E-Lab

www.re-lab.net
Art+Communications – that's the main slogan of E-Lab. This site provides information on many media art institutions – like Sounds OPEN Systems, Multimedia Center Riga, Latvian Academy of Arts and Latvian Artists' Union.

Latnet

www.lanet.lv
Information provided by Latvian Academic Network.

LATNET Art Gallery

www.gallery.lv/
Virtual gallery that welcomes all artists interested in collaboration with the gallery.

Riga This Week

www.eunet.lv/Riga

A web page of a monthly events magazine.

Agency Riga 800

www.riga800.lv

A special agency established to celebrate the 800th anniversary of the founding of Riga. Provides information on events planned for 2001.

Riga in Your Pocket

www.inyourpocket.com

A web page of a monthly events magazine.

Baltic Times

www.lvnet.lv/baltictimes/artsent.htm

A website on news and current affairs.

Media and Books

English and American newspapers and magazines are not readily available. There are a few outlets for English books, one of the best is **Globuss** at 26 Valnu Street and **Janis Roze** at 85a Elizabeth Street. The Baltic Times, a weekly newspaper, is a good way to be informed about the country.

Valters un Rapa, 24 Aspazija boulevard

NIGHT CLUBS

There is an exciting and varied nightlife for all ages.Visitors can watch caberet or dance until dawn. The added attraction is that the city is celebrated for the special beauty of its girls who are tall and statueqe and outnumber the men two to one. The choice of Nightclubs is wide, only a small number are mentioned here.

BIG POINT

109 Vrivibas iela, ☎ 7370360, www.bigpoint.lv, Fri, Sat 22.00-06.00. Admission 1-3Ls. Russian and European radio hits.

CLUB ESSENTIAL

2 Skolas iela, Thr, 23-06.00, Fri, Sat 23.00-08.00, Sun 23.00-05.00,

www.essential.lv. Admission 2-5Ls.
Club Essential offers two halls with six bars, and is spread over three floors. In the main dance hall enjoy Europe's most played music. Qualitative sound and the newest light effects are developed by the best experts of the Baltics. R&B is played in the chill-out zone.

DEPO

32 Valnu iela, 7211374, depo@klubsdepo.lv. Big venue with upgraded facilities such as improved ventilation and chill-out spaces. For those who prefer underground electronic music and alternative rock, serious house and techno – this is definitely the Club. Concerts start at 21.00, Wed-alternative Latvian bands live, Thr – radio SWH live projects, Fri – electronic house, disco, Sat – house, techno, drum and bass.

NAUTILUS

8 Kungu iela, ☎ 7814477, fax 7814455, cap@nautilus.lv, www.nautilus.lv. Admission: 1-5Ls. Nautilus is designed like a futuristic submarine and is mostly submerged under the energetic waves of house and progressive music. The Nautilus space contains four zones of entertainment/relaxation: main dance floor with Ballantine's bar' chill-out zone; Absolut vodka bar; Remy Martin-bar.

PULSE

2 Citadeles iela, http://pulse.808.lv, Wed, Thr from 21.00 (1Ls admission) Fri, Sat 22.00-05.00. Admission 2-3Ls. Discounts with flyers and age restriction 18 yrs. Alternative underground electronic dance music, live performances, industrial design, DJs play vinyl-drum'n bass, industrial, techno and trance.

VOODOO

(in Reval House Latvija) 55 Elizabetes iela, ☎ 7772355, 21.00-05.30. Admission: 6Ls. Three different dance floors, decked out with African masks, the main interior elements are dark wood and colour red. The nightclub caters for a mature clientele, with mellow European music and Russian hits, whereas DJs in the disco try to encourage their patrons to swing to the R'n'B and House tunes. The scarcely dressed go-go girls will definitely heat up the atmosphere. Chill out in the Vanilla Lounge, which serves cocktails based on Absolut Vanilla vodka.

ALCATRAZ (Pelican Pub)

88 K. Barona iela, ☎ 7294984, www.alcatraz.lv, 11.00-01.00, Fri, Sat 11.00-04.00. The staff scurries about in prison wardrobe managing to remain cheerful whilst bidding their time. Graffiti paintings that adorn the walls. Live country, blues and rock'n'roll Thursday, Friday, Saturday.

CETRI BALTI KREKLI Literature & music club (4 White Shirts)

12 Vecpilsetas iela, ☎ 7213885, 12.00-02.00, Fri, Sat 12.00 – last guest. Admission 1-4Ls.

Rising and well-known Latvian bands perform live and all music played is 100% Latvian.

HAMLETS

5 Jana Seta, 2nd floor, ☎ 7229938, 19.00 – last guest.

Inspired by Shakespeare' play, this club/theatre is run by the Latvian Actors' Association and presents a variety of shows and plays by a host of well-known actors, musicians and dancers. Fri or Wed improvisation theatre – just check their calendar. Every Mon, Fri and Sun evening from 21.00 until 23.30, the Swing Time Ensemble proudly presents the Swing Time Jazz Club

GOLDEN BAR

33/35 Gertrudes iela, mob ☎ 25505050, 17.00-07.00, www.goldenbar.lv.

After an intense night of dancing, you'll be glad to find this quieter place, where you can rest your ears and feet, talk without having to shout, and wind down from stress and noise in an elegant atmosphere. Should you still want to dance – music mixes from the Café del Mar, Buddha Bar and Costes will keep you awake.

PULKVEDIM NEVIENS NERAKSTA

(Nobody writes to the Colonel) 26/28 Peldu iela, ☎ 7213886, 18.00-02.00, Tue, Wed, Fri, Sat 18.00-05.00. Admission Tue, Wed, Sat 1Ls, Fri 2Ls. Named after Gabriel Garcia Marquez' novel and artistically designed, the "Colonel" is definitely a favourite and one of the hippest hang-outs for the alternative crowd. The music varies from punk to fusion and acid jazz. Check the programme at the entrance for an insight on the DJ's demeanour.

PUPU LOUNGE

14 Marstalu iela, Wed, Thr, Fri, Sat, 12.00-last guest, www.pupu.lv. Happy hour 17.00-20.00 – buy one cocktail, get one free. Inspired by the fashionable lounge-style restaurants in New York and Milan. "Pupi" in Latvian means tits, and you definitely see them everywhere: on the wall paper and live – sexy waitresses show off their cleavage. Order a dance with a waitress for 200Ls, fire any of the employees for 5000Ls or, yes, you can even destroy the bar for a 'mere' 500 000Ls. DJ sets from Wed to Sat. Chill-out zone and dance floor on the second floor. Don't leave without trying the special house cocktail Better Than Sex.... But is it really? Bachelor parties are not welcome in this exclusive club! Non-locals can only get in if you are accompanied by a girl.

Opening Times

The opening times for shops, museums and banks are similar to other European cities. Shops are open from 8am to 7pm and closed on Sundays. Museums usually close on Monday but specific times are given in each case.

Passports/Visas

Visitors from Europe and USA do not require a visa to enter Latvia. Visas are required by visitors from Canada, Australia, New Zealand and Israel.

Phrases

Hello, Hi!	Sveiki
How are you?	Ka iet?
Yes	ja
No	ne
OK	Labi
Thank you	paldies
Please	ludzu
Good morning	labrit
Good afternoon	labdien
Good evening	labvakar
Left	Pa kreisi
Right	Pa labi
Where?	Kur?
When?	Kad?
How much is it?	Cik tas maksa?
Do you speak English?	Vai jus runajat angliski?
I don't understand	Es jus nesaprotu
Bill, please	Rekinu, ludzu
Have you film?	Vai jums ir filma?
I'm not well	Nejutos labi
Please call a doctor	Ludzu,

	izsauciet arstu
Hotel	viesnica
Bread	maize
Coffee	kafija
Tea	teja
Vegetables	darzeni
Beer	alus
Open	atverts
Closed	slegts
Street	iela
Square	laukums
Great Britain	lielbritanija
Pharmacy	aptieka
Phone	telefons
Doctor	arsts
Flu	gripa
Film	filma

Bus	autobus
Taxi	taksometrs
Train	vilciens
Tram	tramvajs
Airport	lidosta
Ticket	bilete
Train Station	dzelzcela stacija
Toilet	tualete
Garage	garaza
Petrol	benzins

Post

Post offices are open from 8 am to 7 pm on weekdays and 8 am to 4 pm on Saturdays. Exceptions are the Central Post Office at 19 Brivibas; 1 Station square and 24 Aspazija boulevard which are also open on Sunday from 8 am until 4 pm. The Central Post office is open until 11 pm on weekdays and until 10 pm on Saturdays and Sundays.

Public Holidays

January 1	New Year's Day
April 2	Good Friday
April 4	Easter
May 1	Labour Day
May	Second Sunday in May is Mother's Day
June 23	Ligo or Midsummer Festival
June 24	O Jani or St John's day
November 18	Independence Day
December 25-26	Christmas and Winter Solstice
December 31	New Year's Eve

Restaurants

Visitors are spoilt for choice, as there are many cheap restaurants. It is a city like Paris where you can eat well for little. Be adventurous and you will only spend a few lats on a meal. I have often done this at the Lido Bistros.

Expensive

Otto Schwarz

(in Hotel de Rome) 28 Kalku iela

☎ 7087623

The exclusive restaurant on the top floor is the place to treat yourself or to have a power breakfast because both the food and the view are first class. All dishes are skillfully prepared from local produce and there is a selection for vegetarians too on the menu. Pot au feu of seafood in crab bouillon and vegetable cake with marinated goat's cheese and wild garlic are examples of the menu. An introduction to the cuisine is the business lunch which is served until 15.00.

Seasons

(in hotel Grand Palace), 12 Pils iela

☎ 7044000

19.00-23.00. Closed Sun. Fine dining in elegant surroundings awaits you at the Seasons. Award winning chefs prepare "seasonal" culinary delicacies and specialties. Selected wines and champagnes. Pick your appetizers and starters from the myriad of dishes available in the menu, but be sure to try the "Peppered deer carpaccio, marinated in wild berries vinegar" for a real gourmet's feast. Also serves oysters!

Vincents

19 Elizabetes iela

☎ 7332634, 7332830, restorans@restorans.vincents.lv, www.vincents.lv

12.00-15.00, 18.00-23.00, Sat 18.00-23.00. Closed Sun. A culinary institution, Martins Ritins has singled-handedly changed the local palates and established an international reputation with his innovative menus. Consequently, heads of state, captains of industry and celebrities gravitate to his restaurant when visiting the city. He uses mainly locally grown organic produce in his dishes. A fine wine list and good sommelier.

Carpe Diem

10/12 Meistaru iela

☎ 7228488

10.00-24.00, Thr, Fri, Sat 10.00-02.00.

If you like jazz and believe that music enlivens your digestion, this is the place for you. International cuisine served in elegant surroundings. Live jazz daily from 19.30-22.30.

Hotel Bergs Restaurant

(in Berga Bazars) 83/85 Elizabetes iela

☎ 7770957

Breakfast buffet 07.00-11.00, dinner 12.00-24.00.

Located in the ultra chic Bergs hotel in the Berga Bazars, this restaurant is one of the best in town. Start with tuna fish tartar with sesame and seaweed salad and proceed with a main course of local saddle of rabbit with rabbit liver pate and cranberry sauce. For dessert, try goat's cheese mousse with vanilla pod, marinated kumquats and raspberry sauce. A good venue for afternoon tea where you can admire the cool Zaiga Gaile interior and the delicious deserts under the glassed-in terrace, seated in a comfortable wicker armchair.

Skonto Zivju Restorans (fish restaurant)

4 Vagnera iela (I-2)

☎ 7210087, 7216713, www.zivjurestorans.lv

Open: 12.00-24.00.

A restaurant which offers seafood in elegant surroundings in a choice of four dining rooms, each in a separate style. You can pick your lobster or trout from the aquaria. Start with the lobster Bisque soup and afterwards have the fillet of sea devil with fresh asparagus and garlic butter and fried snails.

Moderate

La Boheme

2a J Alunana iela

☎ 7321938,6481581

12.00 – 23.00, Sun 12.00-20.00

La Boheme is a clever division of a trendy café and a fine dining restaurant. Light meals such as salads, soups, pastas and sandwiches are available on one hand and a selection of sophisticated dishes such as rack of lamb in Pinot Noir and black currant glazed duck in the elegant establishment on the other hand. A place to enjoy a leisurely meal or a snack and some beer. A lunch menu is available from 12.00-15.00.

Gastronome

At MC2 complex, 68a Krasta

☎ 7019619. Also in Reval Latvia hotel ☎ 7228053, 7772356

The restaurant is a special experience because you first get a preview of deli food through their unique delicatessen market. This is the Latvian equivalent to the famous Harrods food hall and should get your taste buds hopping. The restaurant is known for its quality food which it does not swathe in sauces and therefore diners can enjoy the original taste. The speciality is fish dishes and fresh oysters from France, tuna and swordfish steaks, scallops, lobster are part of the seafood selection found here. But carnivores are not neglected as meat dishes are also available.

Dada

16 Audeju iela

☎ 7104433, 10.00-24.00, www.sushi.lv.

A fun place where anarchy reigns supreme! Each waiter's uniform is an artwork on its own and no matching cutlery is in sight on the tables. The chief innovation is the cuisine which is based on the 'food market' concept that requires the clients to pick their own selection of food whether it be meat, fish, vegetables and sauces and watch while their food is cooked. There are also at least three mains in a separate menu, as well as desserts.

Macaroni Noodle Bar

17K Barona iela

☎ 7217981, www.sushi.lv

12.00-24.00. Also on 14 Audeju iela.

One of the trendiest noodle bars, it has minimalist decor and furnishings. Pasta's aplenty both Italian and the eastern variety. There's Thai rice noodles with pork and shrimps as well tortellini with wild mushrooms and gorgonzola sauce.

Melnie Muki (The Black Monks)

1 Jana Seta

☎ 7215006

12.00-02.00.

The main feature of this restaurant is the fusion of the bare medieval brick with modern polished wood and textiles. The chef was once the private cook of former president Ulmanis. Fajitas with turkey meat and fish dishes are most popular.

Raibais Balodis

(in Konventa Seta hotel), 9-12 Kaleju iele

☎ 7087580

The restaurant which is in the heart of the Old Town is a romantic venue for dining and offers a variety of international dishes. There are unusual combinations that include chicken liver, for example, in the 'coloured pigeon' salad and as fritters with blanched asparagus in smoked breast of pork, spinach and balsamico crème. It is also a place to enjoy a relaxed breakfast from an unlimited buffet.

Red Fred

62 Dzirnavu iela

☎ 7365113, www.sushi.lv

11.00-24.00, Sat, Sun 11.00—02.00.

The restaurant, which is in a former fire station is a place where you can enjoy beer and food that goes with it like huge steaks, snacks, chips and soups. The meals are served by attractive "fire-women" and there is live jazz/blues every evening.

Tiramisu

32 Gertrudes iela

☎ 7312218

11.00-23.00, Sat 12.00-23.00, Sun 12.00-22.00.

A small popular Italian restaurant, in trattoria style, with tiles and mirrors, is a haunt of the local intelligentsia and foreign embassy people. Reserve a table if you want to dine on Friday nights. Their list of Italian wines are second to none with some 100 wines from every region.

Kabuki

46 Terbatas iela (entrance from Martas iela)

☎ 7842728, www.sushi.lv, 12.00-22.00.

14 K. Barona iela (entrance from Elizabetes iela. Also on the sushi bar has moderately priced cuisine compared to the Sumo restaurant which has the same owners. Dine on classic Japanese dishes in a modern setting. The outlet on Barona iela is more spacious and features a food conveyor system.

Sumo

8 Kungu iela

☎ 7503244, www.sushi.lv

Open: 12.00 – 23.00.

Comprehensive menu of sushi,sashimi, tempura, yakitori and noodles, dishes which can be accompanied with the traditional sake or beer. minimalist lighting and décor. Staff provide friendly and attentive service.

Arbat

3 Vagnera iela

☎ 7214057

12.00-24.00.

Elegant restaurant in rich, colourful style, serving top Russian cuisine. Return to the period of the Tsars with the fish-soup – made of sturgeon, pike perch and vodka. Fresh homemade pelmeni (meat dumplings) are also served.

Lido

76 Krasta

☎ 750 4420 www.ac.lido.lv

Also at 90 Brivibas, 54 Gertrudes, 65 Elizabetes iela and Lido Spice at 29 Lielirbes.

No visit to Riga would be complete without dining at a Lido restaurant. There is a fabulous selection of Latvian food at low prices. Although, they are self service establishments, barbecued meat and fish is cooked while you wait. The flagship at Krasta street is one of the largest log cabins in the world with the biggest buffet table anywhere. There is a vast cellar with a restaurant and two bars which serve beer brewed on the premises. This a place for families particularly at weekends when there are special activities for kids. Another place that caters for kids is Lido Spice which has two-storey castle surrounded by an electric go-kart track.

Bars and Cafes

Skyline Bar

(in Reval Hotel Latvija) 55 Elizabetes iela, 26th floor

☎ 7772222

15.00-02.00, Fri, Sat 15.00-03.00.

The only cocktail lounge on the 26th floor of the tallest hotel in the city. A trendy and urban watering place, it offers a casual atmosphere, cocktails, an original menu combined with the best view in the city. The comfy sofas with plush cushions engender lively conversations. Enjoy the live DJ performances every Fri and Sat, when the hipsters of Riga gather.

Teatra Bars

26 Lacplesa iela

☎ 7282662

This is the place where actors hang out as the New theatre is across the street. It gets lively around midnight when others close down.

Cuba Café

15 Jauniela

☎ 7224362

Open: 12.00-02.00, Fri, Sat 12.00 – last guest, Sun 12.00-24.00.

Happy hours 17.00-20.00 – buy one cocktail, get one free. Warm up your nights in Riga with some caipirinhas (try also the caipirovska and cipirissimo versions) in this bar with character and conveniently located in the Dome Square. As the name of the establishment indficates, only Latino music prevails with DJ sets on Thursday, Friday and Saturday evenings.

Galerija Istaba (art shop and café)

31a K Barona iela

☎ 7281141.

Gallery 12.00-20.00. Closed Sun. Café 12.00-24.00. Closed Sun.

A combo of art and food. The first place in Riga where you can buy your art piece on the ground floor and contemplate your purchase in the café above. There is a selection of souvenirs and art objects for interior decoration made by Latvian artists. The upstairs café which is decorated in a 'grunge student style' offers customers food according to their likes and budget which is up to 5 lats. Be warned there is no menu. A very bohemian place!

Tea Club Goija

1a Strelnieku iela

☎ 7333370

Open: 11.00-02.00. Fri, Sat 11.00-05.00.

The interior is inspired by Moroccan taste. Slippers are provided and customers have the possibility of lying on the sofa, listening to slow tempo music in a quiet central location. The atmosphere is so cosy that it feels like a friend's place. Free internet.

Apsara Tea Rooms

22 Skarnu iela

☎ 7223160

Open: 11.00-23.00.

Also at Elizabetes iela and 2a K.Barona iela. Original décor in European style with antique furniture, a glamorous crystal lamp and an original fire place, but the basement is a mix of Arabian and Indian soft cushion lounge style, where you can enjoy a tea ceremony (Chinese or Japanese) and Turkish delights. Check out the bathroom with its "wisdom graffiti".

Emihla Gustava Shokolahde

(in Berga Bazars) 13/VI Marijas iela

☎ 7283959

Open: 10.00-22.00.

Also 24 Aspazijas bulv. A café in the old Vienna style that produces delicious hand-made chocolates, 30 different styles from truffles to pralines. The manufacture occurs behind the glass wall, so customers can watch the process. Some products are made from ancient recipes of the famous historical confectioner Emil Gustav, and only with high quality Belgian ingredients.

Kanela Konditoreja (Cinnamon Bakery)

(in Berga Bazars) 84-32a Dzirnavu iela

☎ 7217170

Open: 09.00-22.00

Here customers can indulge in both sweet and savoury tastes. There is a good selection of home-made pastries, cookies and cakes with no added preservatives and an aroma of cinnamon, chocolate and coffee pervades the place enough to remind you of your mother or grandmother's kitchen. One of the specialties is Sachertorte, of which there are several recipes and this is one of the best, as well as savoury cakes such as peppermint-cheese and spinach. Bread with olives and basil among other varieties are available.

Osiriss

31 K.Barona iela

☎ 724 3002

Open: 0800-2400;Sat-Sun 1000-2400.

It is the favourite meeting place of locals for over a decade and where one can find a cross section of Riga's society of politicians, artists, businessmen and intelligensia. A selection of tasty dishes for breakfast, lunch or dinner are served. The relaxed ambiance is popular with visitors too.

At the seaside, Jurmala

Here you can eat well, particularly fish dishes, which are freshly caught or smoked. A great place for a picnic is on the Talsu road, about 15 minutes outside Jurmala where fishermen sell smoked fish.

Moderate

Orient Sultan
Majori, 33 Jomas
☎ 776 2082
Eastern European dishes as well as fish are served in this popular venue. It is the prime place to watch promenaders.

At Gabriel's
Majori, 31 Jomas
☎ 776 4268
An interesting Armenian menu.

Slavic Restaurant Club
☎ 776 1401
Majori, 57 Jomas.
Russian cuisine, live music and disco at the weekends.

Juras Zakis
Bulduri, 1 Viembas
☎ 775 3005
Near the beach, and besides fish dishes they have cheesecake for dessert. Popular.

Restaurant of the hotel Lielupe
64/68 Bulduri prospekts, Bulduri
☎ 775 2755
Located on the 10th floor with a good view.

Zem Buram
37/8 Vidus prospekts, Bulduri
☎ 775 5127
Cosy atmosphere and delicious European cuisine.

Shopping

The best buys are amber, linen and vodka. Latvia has been known since ancient times as a supplier of amber, that remarkable translucent fossil gum from extinct coniferous trees which is trawled from the sea during autumn, after storms. The range of amber varies from many shades of brown to a light, milky white hue which is prized by the locals. Some translucent amber is embedded with insects and as a resin it is used for its curative properties. You can still find evidence of how it occurred, as the coastline, even in Jurmala, has pine trees growing on the edge of the beaches.

Linen is another traditional product as the country has long been a producer of flax from which the fabric is woven. Bed linen and tablecloths are popular, inexpensive items.

Vodkas are one of the best bargains and both plain and other varieties such as blackcurrant are available. The local company Latvijas Balzams produces its own brands such as Monopols, Rigas Originalis and Kristaldzidrais according to classic Russian technology as well as Stolichnaya. Its brands are organic as the company only uses grain, alcohol, water and sugar with no chemicals.

Incidentally, its other famous product is Black Balsam which is termed as a liqueur but originated from ingredients placed on wounds because of their excellent healing properties. It is used by the locals as a cold cure or in coffee and as a topping on ice-cream.

Other interesting souvenirs include handmade wooden toys, antiques, Soviet memorabilia, icons, leather goods and tinned sprats.

For tourists interested in shopping per se, there are shops in Riga and a shopping centre which is unique to the city and worth a visit. Among the shops are Garage, Gastronome, Stenders, Ballers, Anemone, Putti and Istaba. The shopping centre happens to be Berga Bazars, a block bounded by Elizabetes street in the west and Dzirnavu street in the east and in which most of the aforementioned shops are located.

Garage

83/85 Berga Bazars

☎ 7288308

The shop, which was a former garage of Justs Karlsons's father, Nikolajs, where he tinkered with his Opel car in the 1930's, has been transformed into a gallery of gifts and artworks of top Latvian artists. It's a place to buy small artworks that can be easily packed into a suitcase and taken back home where they can be admired by both friends and family. Here you will find the 'linen Queen', Laima Kaugure, whose Studija Naturals collection not only includes bed and table linen, curtains, clothing, shawls and accessories but handmade in a contemporary way in different colours and mixed with wool, silk and metal. Franceska Kirke's artefactory collection is into emotional gifts, those that evoke nostalgia for example, old postcards, music, books, tar soap bars, perfume and pastry cutters to make gingerbread men and women.

It's cool to buy a gift from Garage – there are even chocolate bars mixed with hemp, chili, cranberries and bread.

Gastronome

At MC2, 68a Krasta iela (☎ 701 9619) and at the Reval Hotel Latvija, 55 Elizabetes iela (7772356/7772391).

Gastronome is a gourmet's double delight! It's a combination of restaurant and food hall. Foodies can browse amongst the thousands of items in the delicatessen market for their favourites whether it be Beppino Occelli's

Piedmontese round cheese or Betjeman and Barton's Pouchkine tea favoured by Prince Charles. Wild pig salami and ham also get a look-in as well as Pierre Oteiza's brand from the Pyrenees is stocked. To obtain the delicate piquant flavour and subtle aroma, the salami is cured in the sun for about five weeks and the ham for 18 months.

But if they are into pasta then they will not be disappointed because they will find Rustichella d'Abruzzo which is made from bronze moulds and dried for 48 hours at a temperature not exceeding 600 that makes it possible to retain all the nutritious and micro-elements. To go with that there are 50 Italian sauces. Once they have made a purchase, it is reasonable to assume that they would have worked up an appetite, either big or small, and can indulge in coffee and patisserie on their way home or enjoy a delicious meal in the restaurant that is well known for among things for its Royal Seafood dish which should be quaffed with Deutz Blanc de Blancs Champagne 1996.

Stenders

(in Berga Bazars) 84 Dzirnavu iela

☎ 6536865

The handmade soaps which are made from high quality, natural ingredients, smell and look so delicious such as the melon, quince and grapefruit that some customers are tempted to eat them and suffer dire consequences! There are over 70 varieties of soaps, bath balls, bath salts that cover a wide choice of aromas from jasmine, lavender, rose, patchouli and lemongrass to ginger, pine needle, linden, eucalyptus, 'wet grass' and oat flake. The range is complemented by bath and sauna accessories like hand scrubs and massage oils. The products can be carefully wrapped with dried rose petals and ribbon to make a perfect present. The most popular soaps are of course, grapefruit, quince cream, strawberry and bath balls with apricot,melon and sugar plum scents.

Ballera Kanceleja

(in Berga Bazars) 13 Marija iela(☎ 7220444) and 16 Audeju iela

In the age of internet where emails reign supreme, it is refreshing to step back into the past and enter a shop where you can buy handmade paper and coloured sealing wax with a variety of different seals. The establishment also has old-world charm with dark, heavy furniture and some antique pieces like an early box camera. Stationery from Italy and Germany is also stocked with ranges of inks, pens and wrapping paper. A special wrapping service is offered . The staff will wrap presents for customers who can choose the paper, the ribbon, the colour of the wax and the type of seal to be used. Unique handmade paper such as a variety coated with spices are on offer and custom-made seals can be ordered.

Istaba gallery

31a K. Barona iela (☎ 728 1141)

Gallery 1200-2000, closed Sunday. Café 1200-2400, closed Sunday.

A Bohemian place where art objects for interior decoration and jewelry by Latvian artists are sold as well as souvenirs of Latvian artists' work. The collection of arty postcards are most unusual and interesting. There is funky café above which overlooks the gallery. No menu is offered but the chef asks each customer what they would like to eat and how much they would like to pay, up about 5 latts, and then produces a meal.

Putti

16 Marstalu iela (☎ 7214229)

email gallery@putti.lv

A luxurious and modernistic setting for Latvian art jewelers and fashion designers. There are lovely chunky pieces of jewelry, each unique and draw inspiration from ethnographic elements of different cultures, the pure and ascetic concepts of the Bauhaus school, postmodernism and natural forms. A variety of materials from gold, silver, precious and semi-precious stones, enamel, pearls are used to create outstanding pieces.

The clothes are couture and fit well with the art jewelry enabling customers to match their accessories with appropriate garments. There is also a range of children's clothing.

Anemone

in Berga Bazars (☎ 724 3333)

A special place which is more than a flowershop, rather a salon as it is decorated with a multitude items you would find in a drawing room that creates a romantic mood. Flowers in Latvia play a significant role in their culture and are presented on every occasion, both to men and women and even by children to their teachers on the first day at school. Expect to be surprised by the floral arrangements and household gifts here.

Telephones

The country has a modern digital telephone system. International calls can be made either from hotels or phone booths with phone cards. Country codes are as follows: UK (44), US (1), Canada (1), Australia (61), Ireland (353), Israel (972).
Emergency calls: Fire 01, Police 02, Ambulance 03.
NB It is illegal to use a mobile phone while driving.

Theatres

There are several theatres in the city but the works performed are either in Latvian or Russian: **Dailes**, **Kabata**, **National**, **New Riga**, **Russian**, **Drama**, **Skature** and **Hamlet Club**. There is also a **Puppet Theatre**, 16/18 K. Barons Street, ☎ 728 5418 and the **Riga Circus**,
4 Merkela Street, ☎ 721 3472.

Time Zones

Latvia is GMT plus 2 hours.

Transport

Riga has a good, comprehensive public transport system that includes buses, trams, trolley buses and trains. It is cheap, costing some 18 santims and tickets can be bought from conductors on board with the exception of trains where they are purchased from kiosks at stations. They run from 5.30am to 12.30am. Taxis are inexpensive too but use orange and black taxis with meters otherwise you may have to haggle over the fare beforehand. For Jurmala, there are regular train services from the Central Station or minibuses.

National and International Rail, Bus and Ferry services

From the Central Station at Station Square, ☎ 1155 (train schedules) or ☎ 723 1181/3397, you can reach Lvov in Poland, Moscow, St Petersburg, Vilnius in Lithuania and Odessa. But check on journey times as trains are slow. Bus connections are widespread and destinations covered include Berlin, Bremen, Brussels, Munich, Munster, Prague, Stuttgart as well as other Baltic states and Russian cities.

The ferry services are limited in schedules and only ply between Stockholm and Travemunde.

Car Rental Agencies include international companies like Avis, Hertz and Eurocar as well as local firms.

Tourist Information

There are three main sources of information on the city and its environs:

Riga

City of Riga Information Centre
6 Ratslaukums
☎ 703 7900
fax 703 7910
www.rigatourism

Old Town Centre

Riga LV 1050 Latvia
☎ (371) 722 1731
Fax (371) 722 7680

Airport Information

☎ (371) 720 7009
www.riga-airport.com

Jurmala Spa and Tourism Information Centre

42 Jomas Street, Majori LV 2015, Jurmala
☎ (371) 776 4276/2167
Fax (371) 776 4672
E-mail jurmalainfo@mail.bkc.lv

Jurmala Tourism information centre

5 Lienes iela, Majori, Jurmala LV-2015
☎ 7147900
fax 7147901
www.jurmala.lv

Latvian Tourist Board

4 Smilsu iela
☎ 722 4664/fax: 7224665
www.tava.gov.lv
4 Pils Square, Riga LV-1050,
☎ /Fax (371) 722 9945,
E-mail ltboard@com.latnet.lv,
website www.latviatravel.com

Riga has a lively cultural life with music, theatre and opera.
There are two sources of information on cultural events, the Information Centres and City Guides published monthly, such as Riga This Week (free).

Bibliography

Agent's Manual 1999. Latvian Tourist Board (Riga 1998)

Art Nouveau Architecture of Riga. Riga 800 Jumava (Riga 1998)

Baedeker's Russia 1914. Baedeker (Leipzig 1914)

Baltic Outlook, March/April, May/June, August/September and October/November 1999

Benn, A & Bartlett, R, *Literary Russia*. Papermac (London 1997)

Einstein, Bergan R, *A Life in Conflict*. Little Brown (London 1997)

Bruders A, Riga, *Madris* (Riga 1997)

Byron, Robert, *The Road to Oxiana*. Picador (London 1997)

Dabolins, A, *Latvia*. Pluse Plus (Riga 1999)

Duncan, A, *Art Nouveau*. Thames & Hudson (London 1999)

Fahr-Becker, G, *Art Nouveau*. Konemann (I Koln 1997)

Feinstein, E, *Pushkin*. Phoenix (London 1998)

Freiberga, Vaira-Vike, *Acta Univeritatis Stockholmiensis – Studica Baltica Stockholmiensia 2*. 1985. Andrejs Pumpur's *Lacplesis Stockholmiensia Journal of Baltic Studies*

Handbook for Travellers. John Murray (1865)

Handbook for Travellers. John Murray (1893)

Hiden, J & Salmon, P, *Baltic Nations and Europe*. Longman (London 1994)

Jurmala This Week, Riga Guide

Kalnina, Dz, *English-Latvian Dictionary*. Avots (Riga 1997)

Kolbergs, A, *Riga*. Lauku Apgads (Riga 1993)

Kolbergs, *A, Story of Riga*, *Old Town and Parks and Boulevards*. Jana Seta (Riga 1998)

Krastins, J, *Riga Art Nouveau*. Metropolis Baltika (Riga 1998)

Lieven, A, *The Baltic Revolution*. Yale (London 1994)

Mandelstam, O, *The Noise of Time*. Quartet (London 1998)

Museums of Latvia. *Latvian Museum Association Puse* (Riga 1999)

Myers, A, *An Age Ago*. Penguin (London 1989)

Newman, E, *Life of Richard Wagner* 1813-1848. Knopf (New York 1966)

Noble, J, William, N & Gauldie, R, Estonia, *Latvia & Lithuania*. Lonely Planet (Hawthorn Australia 1997)

O'Brien, J, Ed New Latvian Fiction, *Review of Contemporary Fiction*. Illinois State (Normal US 1998)

Petersons, R & Naudis, A *A, Architectural Heritage of Jurmala*. (Jurmala Municipal Council 1998)

Radcliffe, M, *A Baltic Story*. R Radcliffe (London 1993)

Riga Downtown, Spring 1999 and Summer 1999

Riga In Your Pocket, Riga This Week

Silis, J, *Latvian-English Phrase Book*. Jumava (Riga 1996)

Tacitus, *The Agricola and the Germania*. Penguin (London 1970)

World Literature Today, *Baltic Literature in the 1990s*, Vol 72:2, Spring 1998

Index

Published by
Landmark Publishing Ltd,
Ashbourne Hall, Cokayne Avenue, Ashbourne, Derbyshire DE6 1EJ England
☎: (01335) 347349 Fax: (01335) 347303 e-mail: landmark@clara.net

ISBN 13: 978-1-84306-313-1
ISBN: 1-84306-313-1

British Library Cataloguing in Publication Data: a catalogue record for this book is available from the British Library.

Print: Cromwell Press, Trowbridge
Cartography & Design: Michelle Hunt

Front cover: Riga Central Station
Back cover Top: Jurmala beach with Lielupe River on the left
Back cover Middle: Dom Church
Back cover Bottom: The Small Guild in Meistaru Street

Picture Credits

Riga Tourism Coordination and Information Centre

Georg Baumanis: 14, 50, 52B, 67TR, 83, 102BR, **Riga Dome:** 22, 50, 67TL, 78
Museum of Decorative & Applied Art: 18, **Irena Bakula:** 39
Small Guild: 56, **Riga 800:** 47, **Information Centre:** 62, **Jurmala Dome:** 63T
Riga Motor Museum: 86, **Museum of Decorative & Applied Art:** 87T, 90
Museum of History of Riga & Navigation: 91, **Rundale Palace Museum:** 102BL, 98, 94, 103, **Araisi Museum:** 102T

DISCLAIMER

While every care has been taken to ensure that the information in this book is as accurate as possible at the time of publication, the publishers and author accept no responsibility for any loss, injury or inconvenience sustained by anyone using this book.